LET'S TALK ABOUT BUSINESS

MIHIR BHATT

The book is dedicated to my parents. They have always supported me in every part of my life. It's because of their love and dedication that I got the opportunity to write this book....

Contents

Contents

Preface

What is Business?

Is it all about making money or a way to influence other people's life or to create revolutionary plans for the mutual growth and development. The ultimate goal of a business is not to earn money but to understand how it impacts and benifits our society. The sole aim of this book is to provide understanding on diffrent concepts of business like finance, accounting, Human Resources, startups etc, with an unique perspective. It provides a roadmap to the uncertain paths of decision making which compels us to revise our understanding of business.

CHAPTER ONE

How to value your business- The Business Quadrant

The cash flow quadrant shows the different methods by which income is generated. Various income generation methods require unique or particular technical skills, training courses and different types of people. And it's a useful tool that led entrepreneurial paths of ambitious people in the search for financial freedom.

The cash quadrant is a very important characteristic of a wealth.

E - employee

is here that most people earn their income (employment jobs).The employee sacrifices time, energy, skills and ideas to his employer in exchange for compensation.Employee income varies through the Commission, but when an employee ceases to work his income taxes.The lack of guaranteed income is the main problem in the E quadrant.The financial freedom of an employee depends on the employer.

S – Self-Employed

The self-employed do work, but for their own job.This quadrant includes restaurant owners, real estate agents, dentists and other industry workers.Many freelancers earn a lot, but like the employee, when they stop working, their income also increases.Self Employed people have much more than an employee, as a result, success usually means working hard and work longer.

B - Business owner

Those in Quadrant B have a cash production machine. Those in S may transition into B owners.For example, a carpenter could possess and work in his joinery business or his business owner could set up a carpentry shop and hire quality carpenters and a manager to run the business.The wealthiest individuals in the world generally own businesses.These include Microsoft's Bill Gates, Amazon's Jeff Bezos, and Tesla and SpaceX's Elon Musk.

I - Investors

Investors hold assets that generate income.This is the passive income quadrant.Investors in this quadrant have generally accumulated money earned in one or more of the other three quadrant, and let the money work and produce even more money for itself. There are thousands of avenues to deploy your money and make it work for you. This is the crescendo of financial freedom

How to value your business?

Valuation is the process of determining the "economic worth" of an asset or company under certain assumptions and limiting conditions and subject to the data available at the valuation date.

Business valuation is a process and a set of procedures used to estimate the economic value of an owner's interest in a business. Valuation is used by financial market participants to determine the price they are willing to pay or receive to affect a sale of a business.

The valuation strategey:-

1. Obtain an in-depth understanding of th business and its ownership intrest.

2. Perform a thorugh financial and qualitive analysis

3. Consider valuation adjustments

4. Reconcile indicated value(s) to arrive at a conclusion of value

5. Present the findings in a report

These factors provide the basis for the evaluation of a business, however it is important to establish a strong business relationship while evaluating your business.

Building a Strong Business Relationship

When it comes to business and sales, building a strong relationship is critical. The stronger your relationship is with your customer, the more likely they will be to refer your business. Every day, make an attempt to build on the relationships you have with your customer. Don't just say hi as they walk in and goodbye as they leave.

The last thing you want to do is make your customer feel like a statistic. Let them know that their business with you is appreciated. Talk to them, strike up a non-business conversation with them. It could involve just about anything, such as the weather, sports, a movie, pets, etc. Non-business conversation puts your customer at ease and gets them talking. The more they talk to you, the more they will open up to you, opening the door for more sales opportunities. Or, you can keep it simple. For starters, get to know you customers by name, then address them by name. Say things such as, "how's it going today?" Or "how was your weekend?" Or "is there anything I can help you with today?" Make your presence known and felt.

Your customer wants to be appreciated, so take a few minutes of your time to show them that you care about them as a customer. Another way to strengthen your relationship with your customer is to keep a Rolodex handy with a list of all of your customers birthdays, anniversaries, and special events. Keep your eyes and ears open for when customers talk about upcoming events in their lives. Such as children's birthdays and graduations. When the appropriate date approaches, send your customer a card, whether it is a holiday card, a birthday card, a graduation card, or a congratulatory card. Just send it. Your customers will appreciate the fact that you remembered them on their special day. This will only strengthen the relationship you already have with them.

There are many reasons to build a strong relationship with your customer, but two of the reasons remain to be key.

One main reason is that customers value and appreciate good customer service. They want the peace of mind of knowing that if something ever happened with their product or service, that they would have you to turn to as their go to person. This is extremely important because your customer will have this in mind when your competition moves in to take them away. As long as you provide excellent customer service, your customer will stick with you. There is no substitute for excellent customer service. Customer service is the most important thing to a customer, even more important than fees'.

The second reason building relationships are so important is because of the referral process. A customer that is treated with respect and provided excellent customer service will most assuredly refer their family and friends to you. Why wouldn't they?

Thus, the most important asset is your customer, so build and strengthen the foundations you have with them. Buy building strong relationships, you will be building your sales.

Communication the Blood of Business

The communication expertise begins by being intentional about communication rather than treating it as an afterthought at the very end of a project or worse after communication problems happen to be proactive about communication we need to make it a habit to ask ourselves seven key questions when faced with any new project or initiative these seven questions reflect the variables that exist in every communication event so what's a communication event you could be making a sales call or presenting at a conference or simply chatting with friends over lunch maybe your company is about to make a major reorganization or maybe it's about to make a minor policy change. Every one of these situations involves communication and those seven variables are at work when we learn to manage these variables we increase the likelihood of communication success you get that sale your conference attendees understand your ideas clearly your friends will feel a more solid relationship with you to the extent that we ignore any of these seven variables we risk miss communication the customer doesn't understand the value of the product and doesn't purchase your conference colleagues think what are you talking about and your friends well they're friends so they give you the benefit of the doubt but repeated miscommunication can leave even our closest loved ones feeling wounded or upset with us

1. Who should receive this news?
2. Who would be the best sender?
3. What is the bottom line message?
4. How the message might be interpreted
5. Do we want or need feedback on the message?
6. What is the best channel?
7. How should time and sequence this message are any other context issues important

To understand these questions and their assesments in the business it is important to understand their framework and application in an organization:-

First, who were the receivers or the people who heard the news did the right people get the message in your situation one of the leading communication problems is assuming that everyone who needs to get a message actually got that message when we take the time to identify each party who should receive a message we'll avoid this common problem

Second, who is the sender of the message was the sender the best person for the job why or why not

Third, what was the intended message did people get enough but not too much information did they know what they were supposed to do in response to the message

Fourth, how was the message interpreted do you think that you and all of the other receivers heard the message in the same way did it mean the same thing to all of you did the sender clarify any aspects of the message that might have caused confusion or emotional upset getting senders and receivers to align their thinking is one of the most challenging aspects of communication

Fifth, How did the message get from the sender to the receiver or what was the channel of communication was it an email a one-on-one a large group meeting maybe a notice on your intranet or a blurb in the newsletter what would have been the best way to get the message from point A to point B

Sixth question is about feedback were receivers asked to share their thoughts on the message if people did give feedback did anyone respond to the feedback or was communication pretty much one way feedback allows us to make sure that the message was received and understood the way that we had hoped finally

Downward communication:- Messages that flow from the top levels of management to the employees throughout the company downward communication is most common but can become distorted if passed through too many people remember the childhood game called telephone one person would whisper something to the next person in the circle who would then whisper it to the next and so on the last person in the circle would say aloud what she heard which was never what the first player had originally said the game was fun and made us all laugh but in business it's not funny try to communicate directly to as many receivers as possible upward communication allows management to learn about problems that only frontline people are privy to when channels are in place for employees to be heard by their leadership they feel more valued upward communication is notorious though for being skewed toward the positive no one wants to give the boss bad news and no one wants to confess when things aren't going well.

Upward messages tend to suffer from a positivist bias you can use opinion surveys Q&A sessions advisory boards Ombudsman hotlines suggestion boxes skip level interviews anything you can think of to encourage upward honest communication in your company horizontal communication is often overlooked yet that dreaded silo mentality begins to grow when departments or units see themselves as independent actors rather than part of a collective system if we can notice a lack of lateral communication you can initiate conversations with people at our level in other departments consider a once-a-week coffee or even just a quick drop by to chat about current projects powerful collaborations often begin as simple conversations. one more group to consider who might be an unintended audience emails are so easy to forward as communicators. we want our message to be received by the intended audience and we need to be aware of unintended audiences so think carefully about who could end up here in your message

It is important to understand that senders of your message should be influential to the receivers. But the real question is what makes a person influential and a good candidate for sending messages people generally influence us if they have some kind of power in our eyes and that power falls into three categories

Legitimate power happens when people comply with a request because the sender has a certain title or position, By fullfiling senior or boss request in a company because the employees respect the position and have to demonstrate that respect through compliance

Reward power refers to behavior motivated because a sender can reward you in some way you follow up quickly with a request from a potential client because he has the power to reward you with new business or just the opposite coercive power happens when a sender can punish you in some way or take away good things in life you follow up quickly with an existing client because he has the power to take his business elsewhere.

Referent power is influenced that happens as a result of credibility if someone else could be more effective passed the torch focus on your purpose and if enlisting someone else to be a spokesperson of your idea would help give the idea wings go for it tap into the influence that will work.

Once we understand and identified who should hear our message we must remember that these people will interpret our message to understand its meaning see the lines drawn through the heads of the senders and receivers. These little lines remind us that no listener is an empty vessel awaiting our message rather people have mental filters. We all have preconceived notions assumptions biases good and bad our unique way of seeing the world your receivers have their own perspectives about you and your message these mental filters can skew how our message is heard and understood. Important communication question to our process what is the bottom line message we've identified our purpose so we know the core idea but we have all of these different receivers with different ways of interpreting the same message so we must learn to focus and frame the idea carefully.

Feedback: Let's start with focus, our first task is to identify the bottom line message what is the one thing your audience must remember when they walk away from your meeting or after they read your memo how can you tell if your communication has a core message a great self check is to share your intended message with a friend or a colleague and ask the question what do you think is the most important takeaway from this speech or email or slide deck if your friend didn't get your bottom line message go back and simplify focus more on the key idea and repeat it more often focusing on one key idea which is challenging as there is so much we need to communicate but it's better to successfully communicate one idea then to unsuccessfully attempt to communicate a bunch of ideas. Therefore the key is to focus your message on particular idea which is framed for our intended audience. By considering the audience's knowledge level possible reactions and reason for listening, frame your message to align with the unique needs of your listeners when we present to executives. The other important aspect is the feedback of the original message which appears to be a one-way communication and turns it into two-way communication. There are dangers with one-way communication one of those dangers is misunderstanding a manager tells an employee to do a certain task but then rushes off to a meeting the employee without a chance to clarify misunderstands the task does it wrong and creates all sorts of problems another danger with one-way communication is low morale a team is told they have to move to a new location and are given no input into the decision they feel unvalued and morale sinks market alignment can go haywire when companies rely on one-way communication to customers a company could decide to offer a new product without getting feedback from its consumer base millions of research and development dollars later the project gets scrapped because customers aren't interested you want to build opportunities for feedback into your organizational communication process to avoid these dangers but there are dangers in seeking feedback as well feedback takes time feedback is dangerous if we ask for input but have no intention of addressing concerns or using the shared ideas morale sinks even lower if leadership pretends to be listening but then isn't really responsive. Thus there are potential dangers of feedback it can slow things down and it creates an expectation that the feedback will be responded to but at the end of the day the benefits far outweigh any potential drawbacks internal feedback can be just as beneficial as customer feedback. The benefits of feedback are undeniable as it improves the organizational communication in companies with two-way communication make it a habit when planning your communication efforts to build in that feedback loop.

Message is our vehicle for communication the channel is the road we choose we begin our choice by exploring the richness of each communication whether it is the media available to us or the richness which is measured by a channel supports immediate feedback provides verbal and nonverbal cues and has a personal focus.

There are several factors to be considered in our channel choice need for permanence makes a written document actually better than a face to face speed and cost also need to be part of our decision and finally affect your leadership team once your Department to know what an outstanding job they did on a project last week which channel would have the better effect a mass email to everyone on the team or a personal handwritten thank-you note to each team member if you need to communicate the seriousness of a new policy are you better off posting a message on a bulletin board or attending a staff meeting to talk about it. Channel makes a difference consider richness permanence speed cost and effect so we've made an intelligent and informed decision when selecting our channel our highway for the message but we may still encounter a few roadblocks in our path.

To understand how a network woks in a company, imagine a situation where a HR director needs to communicate a time-sensitive change in the benefits package to all employees the message starts with a face-to-face visit to the vice president's who are in turn to tell departmental directors who in turn are to tell unit supervisors who in turn tell their staff good plan unless one of those directors also had ten other messages to communicate to her supervisors who were now on overload and another director communicated the message but two of the supervisors were on vacation so didn't pass the message along to their staff some staff members don't have a reporting line to any of those vice presidents

Communication is all one-way and when some employees have heard the message and others haven't the rumor mill kicks in as it inevitably will, when people experience a communication vacuum the grapevine which is the rumor mill is fascinating. it's an informal network of communication that often moves faster than the formal channels but isn't always as accurate rumors and misinformation can spread rapid-fire hence that great line a lie can travel halfway around the world while the truth is still lacing up its boots we can't dictate an order to stop using the grapevine rather we can attempt to limit its damaging effects by sharing a wealth of information in the formal channels when people aren't thirsty for information they're less inclined to participate in rumor spreading concede that the rumor mill exists attempt to understand its nuances and use it when appropriate to supplement the slower formal channels meetings are a channel that we rely on heavily in the workplace more.

The next aspect of a communication is to improve the efficiency of the meetings.

First make a minor adjustment to your agenda to improve the efficiency of your meetings most agendas look something like this strategy realignment quarterly sales regional marketing plans suggest that you add an objective to each agenda item like this determine the next steps for strategy realignment report quarterly sales brainstorm regional marketing plans people prepare and interact differently if they are listening to brainstorming about or acting on deciding on an issue let them know in advance what mental space to be in as they enter the meeting then add a time frame to each agenda item the time frames allow people to gauge how much sharing is appropriate.

If we reach the end of the allotted time and the team has not finished that item you can simply ask do we want to continue this discussion and eliminate some other agenda item or can we in the next two minutes wrap this up teams frequently realize that they are belaboring a point and will choose to wrap up and move on suddenly naysayer are ready for a vote people full of conversation are ready to be quiet and you move on. Therefore, these different business segments play an important role in developing and in the growth of a business where the communication becomes the life blood of a business.

Is Diversity Important in a Business?

What exactly does it mean to have a diversity where diversity is to work with different people from different age groups different backgrounds different cultures caste communities etc well gone are the traditional days wherein people had only a one-track mind of sitting and working together with people that they got along with nowadays the dynamics are changing so quickly that you need to become somebody who can jell with people from diverse cultures and diverse backgrounds this is what diversity is all about well there are certain elements of workplace diversity which means that you have to work with people from different age groups different genders different people who come from different income background the education also differs their race their physical disabilities at times corporates also hire people who probably are disabled and probably on a wheelchair or there could be having certain other disabilities the entire idea of elements of diversity is to make sure that you work with people on an equal footing on all of these well certain other diversities and elements are personalities you might be working with people from different personality sexual orientation the ethnicity geographical node locations as well could be different parental status an marital status could also deform well friends with such a diverse elements of workplace diversity it only makes sense that you have a very broad out view of things and people that you work with it's very important to be flexible and adaptable and not be rigid with your own way of thinking about such whenever you're working with diverse people now there are certainly many benefits of working in a workplace which has such diversity:-

First benefit is that you tend to have mutual respect well workplace diversity fosters mutual respects among the team members different cultures and age groups bring different dynamics to the table and employees start to trust and gain respect for each other it's very important whenever you're working with diverse set of people you need to have mutual respect for them.

The **second** one is conflict resolution well when you are having a workplace which are having people from different mindset and cultures and diversity is there it's important to know how to resolve your conflict in fact you've become very mature at handling conflicts in a professional manner

The **third** is business repetition another benefit of workplace diversity is when an organization makes an effort to build a diverse workforce it acquires respect and profitability fair employment practices and diverse workforce attracts more and more qualified people so as an organization or as a business you gain a positive repetition in the market for the same well job promotion also is one of the benefits of having a workplace diversity when you work in an organization which respects and encourages diversity you become globally accepted and hence to find a job in any global competitive market becomes easier when you've worked with people from different cultures and communities

Cognitive diversity which is about differences in perspectives and insight and the models in heuristics we deploy to make sense of the world around us and also perhaps differences in thinking styles some people are quite analytical thinkers and others more holistic collective intelligence. This can be understood through:-

1) A psychological point- consumers are attracted unconsciously to people who think like us when people are mirroring our perspective back to us it makes us feel smarter it validates our worldview when it's a simple task that's fine any one person has a solution you surround yourself with like-minded others you are able to deliver the solution but as the complexity increases and no one brain is sufficient to solve the problem.

2) When an individual is attracted to people who think in the same way you're getting no uplift at all in collective intelligence and by mirroring each other's perspectives you become more confident about a solution that might be gravely mistaken. This is why cognitive diversity is so important and will become the key feature of competitive advantage.

However, the most important benefit is increased exposure well when you are meeting or dealing with people from diverse backgrounds it definitely helps you to become more exposed towards things and you might you know be working with people have different mindset different opinions and different way of working all together it's always good because it adds on to your profile and you get to learn from different people at the same time well as a person who has to manage people from different diverse backgrounds there are certain strategies which will help you to manage them better the number one strategy is you need to prioritize communication well it becomes important because you are dealing with people from so many different cultures and backgrounds and diversity it is only important that communication should be clear crisp and concise the next one is you need to treat every employee as an individual you need to encourage them to work in diverse teams you need to become somebody who's open-minded flexible and adaptable towards working with different set of people you need to observe carefully and listen to their problems that they might be facing and you need to make sure that you keep them motivated while they're performing at their workplace well friends workplace diversity is something which is a must-have if you want to join anywhere in the globe any company which has a mindset of having diverse people in their teams is definitely an add-on to work with it is just not for the benefit of the company but the employees also gain exposure to different working styles of people from different geographical backgrounds people from different cultural backgrounds ethnicity age or gender make the workplace a box of so many different ideas and there is so much of learning which happens because people have their own set of ways of thinking and ideologies and opinions hence it always makes a challenging to work in a workplace which has diversity

CHAPTER TWO

Law and Tax

Law is the principles and regulations established in the community by some authority and applicable to its people whether in the form of legislation or of customs and policies recognized and enforced by judicial decision any written or positive rule or collection of rules prescribed under the authority of the state or nation as by the people in its constitution by law and statutory law. The controlling influence of such rules the condition of society brought about by their observance in maintaining law and order so any rule of action or any system of uniformity and that is the definition of law there are two divisions:-

The first division is law which is promulgated and enforced by state that is the first division meaning to say

1) Laws that are enforced by our government

2) Law which is not promulgated and enforced by state

But how are these laws diffrent from Business laws:-

Business law encompasses all of the laws that dictate how to form and run a business. This includes all of the laws that govern how to start, buy, manage and close or sell any type of business. Business laws establish the rules that all businesses should follow. A savvy businessperson will be generally familiar with business laws and know when to seek the advice of a licensed attorney. Business law includes state and federal laws, as well as administrative regulations. Let's take a look at some of the areas included under the umbrella of business law.

The Indian Contract Act, 1872 prescribes the law relating to contracts in India. The Act was passed by British India and is based on the principles of English Common Law. It is applicable to all the states of India except the state of Jammu and Kashmir. It determines the circumstances in which promises made by the parties to a contract shall be legally binding and the enforcement of these rights and duties.

The Act as enacted originally had 266 Sections, it had wide scope and included.

General Principles of Law of Contract- Sections 01 to 75

Contract relating to Sale of Goods- Sections 76 to 123

Special Contracts- Indemnity, Guarantee, Bailment & Pledge- Sections 124 to 238

Contracts relating to Partnership- Sections 239 to 266

Indian Contract Act embodied the simple and elementary rules relating to Sale of goods and Partnership. The developments of modern business world found the provisions contained in the Indian Contract Act inadequate to deal with the new regulations or give effect to the new principles. Subsequently, the provisions relating to the Sale of Goods and Partnership contained in the Indian Contract Act were repealed respectively in the year 1930 and 1932 and new enactments namely Sale of Goods and Movables Act 1930 and Indian Partnership act 1932 were re-enacted.

At present the Indian Contract Act may be divided into two parts

Part 1:deals with the General Principles of Law of Contract Sections 1 to 75

Part 2:deals with Special kinds of Contracts such as

(1)Contract of Indemnity and Guarantee

(2)Contract of Bailment and Pledge

(3)Contract of Agency.

1. **Offer 2(a)**:- When one person signifies to another his willingness to do or to abstain from doing anything, with a view to obtaining the assent of that other to such act or abstinence, he is said to make a proposal.

2. **Acceptance 2(b)**:- When the person to whom the proposal is made, signifies his assent there to, the proposal is said to be accepted.

3. **Promise 2(b)** :- A Proposal when accepted becomes a promise. In simple words, when an offer is accepted it becomes promise.

4. **Promisor and promisee 2(c)** :- When the proposal is accepted, the person making the proposal is called as promisor and the person accepting the proposal is called as promisee.

5. **Consideration 2(d)**:- When at the desire of the promisor, the promise or any other person has done or abstained from doing or does or abstains from doing or promises to do or to abstain from doing something such act or abstinence or promise is called a consideration for the promise. Price paid by one party for the promise of the other Technical word meaning QUID-PRO-QUO i.e. something in return.

6. **Agreement 2(e)**:- Every promise and set of promises forming the consideration for each other. In short agreement= promise + consideration

7. **Contract 2(h)**:- An agreement enforceable by law is a contract.

Therefore, there must be an agreement and it should be enforceable by law.

Tax:

Every government wants a more number of taxpayers, Honest taxpayers, and Regular tax payments. There shall not be any inconsistency One way to ensure this is to make the law and compliances. more simple and organized and introducing online portals. That's what the government has already been doing

But the Government has thought of another way, as in India out of 133 cr only 1.4 crore peoples pay the taxes. So the government thought to remove the fear factor of tax from people's minds.Most people pay income tax out of fear. The government thought that if we remove this fear then maybe. more people come forward to disclose their income and pay their income tax comfortably

That is exactly what this Transparent Taxation Scheme wants to achieve. So let's first see the present scenario. Every taxpayer has to give tax on his income and for this, he files an income tax return mentioning all of his income. The Income Tax department checks the credibility of this return. For this, they use two types of tools

The first one is Form 16 which is used in an employee's case in which your employer mentions how much TDS has been deducted, And you tell him about your investments so that he can deduct TDS accordingly your allowances, your Rank and HRA, etc, and all this information goes to the income tax department. Second tool is this Section of Finance Act 2014. 'Obligation to furnish statements of financial transactions or reportable account' In shot Statement of Financial Transaction, SFT. Under this government has the power to direct big financial institutions like Banks and even companies to provide the information of any large financial transaction made by them to the government in the specified format.

The government appoints an officer to scrutinize your account and to look for anything fishy. If the officer finds something suspicious then he can ask for additional information, like Proof of expenditure, invoice etc. If the officer is still not satisfied & puts some charges over you to pay some amount of tax. Then you can appeal against it to the income tax commissioner.

If an assessment gets a notice from the Income-tax office then he has to physically meet the assessing officer which may lead to some adjustment situations. When the taxpayer directly interact with assessing officer, corruption begins. When the two will face each other any of record conversation between them, will not be known by the department. This gives rise to corruption.

Reforms introduced in the Budget 2022-23:

The first reform is the faceless assessment and faceless appeal. Under this new system, a central computer will analyze your filed returns and match the entry in the SFT against your PAN card and check whether entries in the form 16 are matching with your returns or not then it will pick some random entries and send them to an assessing officer. Now this assessing officer would neither be of your city, nor would he know who he's scrutinizing and how the documents will be marked and changed with DIN (Document Identification Number).These faceless assessments are running live from 13th August 2020. And you can also do faceless appeal, if you are not satisfied with this online assessment or if an officer has put a charge over you. All this process would be online and all names would be confidential.

The second benefit is Taxpayer charter. Charter means when a sovereign body transfer the power to a lower body. So, what powers this reform offers to the taxpayer of our country?

The government says that an income tax officer cannot harass you unless he is having some solid proof against you and he can't order for Raid or seizer or scrutiny without solid proof. All your assessments and appeals would be faceless, unless you have committed a major crime, like money laundering or international fraud. Everything would be in a time-bound manner. Whether it's a pending refund or a pending appeal. So, this is all the government has to offer under taxpayer charter, but this charter comes with some responsibilities as well. It is the responsibility of a citizen to use all these powers honestly. Through these government is trying to plug in all those things which could be fabricated by the taxpayers, which is the biggest move taken by the government in 2022.

CHAPTER THREE

What the F with Finance?

Through decades of technological advances, the earliest attempts to make finance more efficient started as early as the 1920s with the introduction of accounting machines and punch cards this was followed by the rise of the mainframe computers that significantly sped up the banking system in the 1950s and beyond the next revolution was the invention of ATM's and credit cards that started being popular in the 1970s another important element of the financial system the stock market started going through a radical transformation manual order entries and loud trading pits started being slowly replaced by computers and algorithms from the 1990s thanks to the growing adoption of the internet the computerization of finance got supercharged accessing bank accounts making wire transfers buying stocks all of these operations were now possible from the comfort of our own houses. The biggest question is why we need something new something better that can address some of these problems and Fin-tech is introduced as a phenomenon that is changing and touching our lives. Fin-tech is not really a new concept even ATM machines at their time were thin tech innovations in the 1960s but what has made fin tech go so unmask is is just the pace of innovation in this space the rate of innovation and the abundance of new technologies which have sprung up everywhere now what is blockchain without going too much into the technology it is like spreadsheets which are distributed around the world on built on the Internet so as opposed to the old system where you would have just one copy of a central ledger, as one can have thousands of these copies of the same ledger and they're all linked together and constantly synced together which makes it cryptographic-ally Therefore, fin-tech is the decentralized finance which comes into play instead of relying on old and inefficient infrastructure decentralized finance or defy leverages the power of cryptography decentralization and blockchain to build a new financial system a system that can provide access to well-known financial services it doesn't matter that counterparts may be in completely different geographic locations with inconsistent laws and regulations on top of this most of d5 protocols can operate with no or minimal human involvement fair as all services are completely permission less and censorship resistant permission less as everyone with a browser and the internet connection can access them there is no document verification no need to provide income statements nationality or race doesn't matter everyone is treated in the exact same way . To overcome these problems, Three moves are especially critical for delivering greater real-time insights and driving speed in workflows and decision-making. Help finance lead in data, Re-imagine the finance operating model with new capabilities, Look beyond transactional activities. Therefore, In achieving the next frontier in finance efficiency and effectiveness will likely require finance executives to shift their thinking from the priorities of the past and laid a foundation stone for the future of finance.

Ethical Concerns In Corporate Finance and ways to overcome It

Finance is considered the lifeblood of any business organization. The finance is needed even those areas where economic activities of any type or prefer according to has to spend and test name something must be there for directing the flow of economic activities and this conduct without any bottleneck finance is the only means which can perform this function.

Money in finance alone cannot lead to economic development, the financial system plays a significant role in bringing about the economic development of any country this is achieved by stimulating the accumulation of capital and by efficient allocation of it if any economy. There are two groups of people:-

1) The savers are those whose current income exceeds the current expenditure
2) The investors are those whose current income is less than the current expenditure

Aspects: The function of the financing system is to establish the bridge between these sailors and the investors and to facilitate the transformation of savings into investment.

The next aspect is the structure of the Indian gentle system the financial system of any country comprises the financial markets and the supporting institutions. The financial market is one in which financial assets are created or transferred financial assets represent a claim to the payment of the sum of money sometime in the future in the financial system consists of the Indian money market and capital market. The distinction between this market is based on the period for which the money is lent and borrowed the money market deals with all transactions in short-term debt with a period of maturity of one year or less whereas the capital market pertains to transactions related to long-term depth with a period of maturity fo one year the Indian financial system consists of financial markets financial institutions financial instruments in financial services first the financial markets the financial market is the place where the financial assets are created or transferred the financial assets represent decline through the payment of a sum of money sometime in future the financial markets may be classified either primary and secondary or more of money market capital market government security markets foreign exchange market.

There is list of ethical principles involved in the businesses:-

The first one is their integrity whenever there is great pressure to do right instead of maximizing profits this principle is tested the executives need to demonstrate courage and personal integrity by doing what think is right they need to fight for their beliefs for these principles they will not back down and hypocritical or experienced

No ethical behavior can be promoted without trust and for trust loyalty needs to be demonstrated the executors need to be worthy of this press who is remaining loyal to the institution's and the person there should be in friendship in the time of adversity and support and devotion for the duty they should not use or disclose personal information this leads to confidence in the organization they should safeguard the ability of professional to make an independent decision by avoiding any kind of influence or conflicts of interest so they should remain loyal to their company and their colleagues when they accept the other employees they need to provide a reasonable time to the firm thus they should refuse to take part in any activity that might take the undue advantage of the form

The honesty the ethical executives are harnessed while dealing with and requires the need to be truthful and do not deliberately deceive or mislead the information to others there should be an avoidance of the partial truth over statements misrepresentation etc. Thus they should not have selective omission by any means possible.

Problems: The principles of ethics involves avoiding the exploitation of consumers do not cheat and exploit consumer with emissions such as artificial price rise and adulteration the next one is avoid profiteering unscrupulous business activities such as whole during black marketing selling banned or harmful goods to earn extra or parent profit must be abided the next one is encourage healthy competition a healthy competitive atmosphere that offers certain benefits to the consumer must be encouraged the next one is ensure accuracy in weighing packaging and quality of supplying goods to the consumers has to be followed the next one is paid tax regularly taxes and other duties to the government must be honestly and regularly paid the next one is get the accounts audited proper business records accounts must be managed all authorized persons and authorities should have access to this the next one is fair treatment to implies third wages or salaries facilities and incentives must be provided to the employees keep the investors informed the shareholders and the investors must know about the financial and other important decisions of the company the next one is avoid injustice and discrimination avoid all types of industries and partially to implies discrimination based on gender race religion language nationality etc should be avoided

However, the major problem faced by the company first is the improper budgets income and expenditures must be properly defined and the company budgets must have the flexibility to accommodate if there are any deviations from the prescribed form. Insufficient working capital maintains proper current and current liabilities management in the company. The revival and monitoring financial projects how to be identified monitored at frequent intervals and if there is any deviation corrective measures have to be followed

How to deal with Ethical Concerns?

First is public finance: The government has the right to collect finances or revenues through taxation and other means and have the authority to use such finance within the constitutional limits

The second one is securities and investment analysis: Investment analysis encompasses all aspects of investment proposal and develops such techniques which can be used by the investors to minimize the risk the third one is International Finance individual business organizations and the government has to face special financial problems when money is used at international level in transacting business activities the third holiest institution and finance this institution vocalized the savings of the individuals channelized them for the efficient investment in the various sectors of the economy the fifth point is financial management this aspect of finance traditionally known as business finance or corporate finance business concerns or all the time facing a lot of problems for searching the optimum method of racing and utilizing the amount of fund needed for operating their economic activities.

The Indian financial system was in a confused or disorderly condition mainly because of the absence of a strong financial institutional mechanism in the country this led the government to realize the necessity of slowly transferring the ownership of some of the important financial institutions from private ownership to stick hundred accordingly the government took steps to establish the new financial institution and to nationalize some of the existing private financial institutions apart from the nationalization of some of the important private financial institutions the government took the initiative in establishing new financial institutions. The provident funds and pension funds were also started by the government which encouraged savings these savings were completely under the control of the government functions of financial institutions the majority function of the financial institutions is to provide the maximum financial convenience to the public by way of go on promoting the overall savings in a more efficient manner so that those in great need get priority in the allotment and the third creating credit and deposit money for facilitating the transaction of trade and distribution in the economy.

Conclusion: Therefore, business ethics comprises all these values and principles and helps in guiding the behavior in the organizations businesses should have a balance between the needs of the stakeholders and their desire to make a profit while maintaining these balances. Many times businesses require doing trade-offs to compact such scenarios rules and principles are formed in the organization this ensures that businesses gain money without affecting the individuals or society as a whole. The ethics involved in the businesses is reflected in the philosophy of the organization when these policies determine the fundamentals of that organization and played in managing the problems associated with ethics in

the corporate world.

Women Blazing Trails in Finance: Thriving the wall of success

While understanding the diffrent aspects of finance it is significant to understand the role of women in the field of business and trading. India has traditionally been a patriarchal society with low participation of women in the economy. But the fact remains that women represent nearly 50 percent of the total population, and it is crucial to encourage women's role in the economy at every level. The entrepreneurial role is limited to large-scale industries and technology-based businesses.

However, women successfully have established co-operative societies such as Parachute and its success rates encourage them to further enhance their participation and engagement. An increasingly large number of women in India are engaged in the informal economy and operating in the small-scale sector, cottage industries, and micro-enterprises. It is estimated that by 2030, roughly two-thirds of the private wealth in first-world countries like the USA, will be held by women. Women are more likely to invest in a way that benefits women. With this model in mind, countries like India should encourage women in putting their money with the women-led businesses or prioritizing investments with companies that have greater gender diversity. As women make up larger percentages of the impact investing asset management team as compared to traditional asset management. In the field of finance, Women are now in positions of management and operations in most large companies. However, they are concentrated mostly in HR and Customer Relations. Many female managers are also in the banking, pharmaceutical and medical industries. Women are also the majority of managers and workers in retail activities. There still exist a "glass ceiling" when it comes to women in senior management positions. While progress has been made there is still a long way to go to achieve equality with their male counterparts. However, Female entrepreneurship can also have a strong impact on the economy and society. Women often create businesses that cater to different clientele as compared to men. This allows them to focus on a different niche that may not have a booming market yet. This can result in substantial economic growth. Approximately 12.3 million American women own their own businesses. This has resulted in an estimated $1.8 trillion boost in the economy per year. It has also led to the creation of over 23 million jobs. As more and more women choose the entrepreneurial life, the numbers will continue to rise. Thus, by supporting women who are embracing this change can not only impact their lives but impact the lives of others. It can have both a positive outcome on the economy and influence others to make those same changes. Women entrepreneurship has already changed the current state of society and will continue to do so in the years to come. It is important for women to recognize this flawed system and really want to achieve financial freedom and thus obtain the same choice as men with money. The hope is that both men and women with choice, will choose partners because of attraction, mutual respect as human beings, and love, not choosing a woman because she's attractive and when she's not, get a younger one or choosing a man because he takes care of her because that is actually a prison. This can only be achieved if women can all get on the same page about what they truly believe success is because as long as there are attractive women running around looking to be taken care of and that is what women respect as the path to success, too many men will be happy to capitalize. India has traditionally been a patriarchal society with low participation of women in the economy. But the fact remains that women represent nearly 50 percent of the total population, and it is crucial to encourage women's role in the economy at every level. At present women's entrepreneurial role is limited in the large scale industries and technology-based businesses. An increasingly large number of women in India are engaged in the informal economy and operating in the small scale sector, cottage industries, and micro enterprises. With proper governmental and societal support, these women can create sustainable, organized and growth-oriented enterprises with a vision. Government policies and regulations regarding business and industry can be formulated with the intent to encourage women entrepreneurs. Another key aspect must be to facilitate the entry of women entrepreneurs into areas where high growth is expected. Special incentives, tax rebates, duty cuts and subsidized land and machinery can be provided to encourage women in emerging sectors. Special recognitions and award can be instituted for women participating in such targeted industry's economic profile.

Therefore, with proper governmental and societal support, these women can create sustainable, organized, and growth-oriented enterprises with a vision. Conclusively, by participating in business, women become more liberated and add value to the business by putting in their hard work and brilliant ideas.

CHAPTER FOUR

E-commerce

E-commerce entity' means a company incorporated under the Companies Act, 1956 or the Companies Act, 2013 or a foreign company covered under section 2 (42) of the Companies Act, 2013 or an office, branch or agency in India as provided in Section 2 (v) (iii) of FEMA 1999, owned or controlled by a person resident outside India and conducting the e-commerce business.

'Inventory based model of e-commerce' means an e-commerce activity where inventory of goods and services is owned by e-commerce entity and is sold to the consumers directly.

Whereas, **'Market place model of e-commerce'** means providing of an information technology platform by an ecommerce entity on a digital & electronic network to act as a facilitator between buyer and seller.

The Legal Aspect:-

The e-commerce industry has grown significantly in the past few years but its significant growth has been accompanied by an increasingly rigid regulatory environment whilst an e-commerce business can be set up easily in less than an hour this leads businesses to forget about the legal aspects. There are several legal issues that one must be aware of to ensure that your business will properly comply with the law

First, is to incorporating your business if you plan to run your business on an online platform such as a website. It is important to first set up a company which involves purchasing or selling. If you fail to set up your company the business activity might be considered outright illegal registering. Your company is more formally called incorporating your business which simply means you're registering your business to be a limited company

Second, is the terms of use and legal policies moving on to the content of your website by including certain key pages on your site you can better protect your online business from future legal disputes.

Terms of use page is also known as terms and conditions these will entail rules and restrictions that must be followed by customers visiting your website having a terms of use section is important for e-commerce websites because they serve as a contract between the visiting customer and the business when they are accessing the website as a business owner you will be able to assume that the customer has agreed to the terms and conditions listed on your online website while having this page is not a legal requirement it will exempt your business from responsibility for damages that your customers suffer after using your products or service this means that the customer continues to use your website purchase your products and are aware of the terms and conditions it will be presumed that they have agreed to the limited liabilities a delivery or shipping policy. If your ecommerce site delivers goods to customers you should have a delivery or shipping policy a delivery policy should state all the important information which relates to the shipping process after an online order is placed this includes details on delivery methods delivery times shipping costs and warranties provided by having a delivery or shipping policy you will have taken precautions for any shipping issues that are likely to occur especially if there are difficult circumstances such as lost packages and damaged products a returns and refunds policy if you offer returns or refunds as part of your business model you should have a return a refund policy that details when and under what circumstances customers are eligible it should also clearly describe the returns process in detail even if you do not offer returns or refunds you should have a no refund policy to inform your customers that all sales are final. This will help your customer during the decision making process before they make an order on your website it also resolves any misunderstandings they might have on return's eligibility a copyright notice you have to protect your content from being copyrighted by visiting customers and competitors you can do this by placing a copyright notice on your website stating that the content is your property it is protected by copyright and trademark law this will inform customers that the content on your website belong to you under the law and thus cannot be taken or copied without permission data privacy and data protection you must remember that customer information used to place an order passes through different security channels as such consumer privacy and data protection are two areas of major concern.

The **e-commerce businesses** are under a legal obligation to protect consumer privacy and to respect their privacy rights online businesses should always have a privacy policy on their website explaining to the customer that their data is being collected and used you will need to state the purpose behind collecting personal data and where that data is transferred you will need a cookie policy to notify customers that their cookies are being collected and to specify what personal data is stored cookie collection is a requirement to access your online store that should also be clearly stated credit card data if you accept online payment any personal data collected through the payment process needs to be protected and secured as an msme you are probably less likely to directly collect and process payments yourself most msme e-commerce businesses license third-party payment gateways for data collection and payment as such e-commerce sites should ensure that they are using reputable payment gateways such as paypal so that they are compliant with different local data protection standards trademarks the scope for copyright issue is widening commerce and therefore alongside a copyright notice online businesses should consider registering trademarks for extra protection a trademark will protect your business content from being used this is extremely important for maintaining your brand image and to prevent visitors from stealing your content or designs with a trademark it becomes illegal for anyone to use your trademark content without authorization and the trademark owner can seek damages if necessary which is important from a public policy perspective and hence require specialized rules and regulations which will safeguard the interest of the consumers against the wrongdoing.

CHAPTER FIVE

Small Business

Owning and maintaining a very successful small business can have its challenges but if you know what you are doing, everything can work out great for you.There are many helpful tips you should learn if you are a small business owner as well. So, by learning these suggestions that you should have the ability to have a very safe and cost-effective future.Knowing how to properly run a small business will bring you and your employees a lot of relief knowing that their positions are stable and secure.Your employees will be much happier as you want, if you do all the right things and play your good cards. Having a small business has its advantages and some of those will be included throughout this article. You need to learn more about what it takes to run a small business successfully so that if you or someone else is interested in opening a small business, will become more knowledgeable about all aspects of it.

A small business can usually run very successfully, as long as you do some management homework first.your own business, as well as talking with other small business owners because the more experienced people could provide you with a large amount of useful information and some suggestions that can almost guarantee the success of your small businesses and longevity. However it requiers a business plan.

The following business stratergies will help you in devising your own busiess plan for your small business:-

No matter how good a communicator you are, you will never be able to convey your vision for the business as successfully as a perfectly put together Business Plan. It provides a clear understanding as to what you want to achieve. It allows you to express your ideas in a clearer manner.

Too many times business owners try to sell their idea verbally and at the end of the interview with the Bank the Manager is none the wiser than he was at the start. I think you can guess the outcome of many of those requests.

A Business Plan will help convince both you and the Bank of the project's feasibility and viability. There's nothing like having all the facts in front of you to clarify the key issues

There is no getting away from the fact that a business owner who plans ahead comes across as being more ambitious and more focused. A well prepared Business Plan demonstrates you have vision and that you know what you want

With numerous ideas floating around in your mind, the pitfalls or stumbling blocks to success are never that visible. A mind buzzing and full of ideas will rarely achieve clarity. A Business Plan forces you to put your ideas down in writing and in an orderly manner. The result of this could be you going in a completely different direction than you initially thought of, or even abandoning your idea altogether.

By checking progress against your Plan, you will be able to spot if you are moving away from your original vision and so you will know what has to be put right.

Every action you take has a consequence, and a Plan helps make these consequences much clearer. Being aware of the possible effect of your chosen direction allows you to plan ahead, leaving you better able to cope with whatever the world of self employment can throw at you. This is one thing that "mental planning" would not achieve

Putting your thoughts on paper may make you realise that you need to do more research on the demand for your product or service. It could also highlight that more investigation on your competitor's products or services is needed. Additional research could help avoid a potentially costly mistake or even uncover a hidden advantage, which you had not seen before.

This Plan will guide you as to how much money is needed to make an idea work. In your mind you may have a rough figure of what you'll have to commit, but until you do a Cash Flow Forecast you may not realise that an overdraft limit will be required, in addition to a loan for your equipment. Therefore, By the time you have finished writing your Business Plan you will have a total understanding of your business; its strengths and weaknesses, the environment it operates in, what could potentially go wrong, and what you can do to ensure your success.

CHAPTER SIX

Technology- How AI will help make better marketing decisions

Technology is the key aspect of modern living whether it is the products or the services, which are all primed by technology, but looking at it from a different perspective technology has always been there. Because technology is an extremely important driver of how we progress.

At present, Marketing represents the 4th largest use of AI concerning resources spent, and the 5th largest industry adopter of AI technology, with around 2.50% of the total industry. Under Artificial Intelligence, computer technologies hold a vital role in helping businesses to connect with their customers as it comes with powerful reporting tools that enable them to gain better insights into customer behavior. All these are presented through an intuitive screen. By gaining powerful customer insights marketers can make fast decisions while optimizing their digital campaigns that target the right audience and helps marketers to make informed decisions through data analysis, natural language processing media buying automated decision making content generation, or real-time personalization's through its key components like machine learning, big data, and analytics the platform AI also provides increased speed of decision-making, especially in response to new data being available or competitive threats emerging, allowing companies to capture the benefits of stronger market positions earlier. These benefits include Identification of missing data, Increased rationality, particularly via removal or reduction of cognitive bias by decision-makers, Creation of a standard basis for decision-making, Incorporation of learning from experience, and Higher quality management of marketing projects. However, With AI technology being more feasible to implement than ever before, we are beginning to see its marketing potential unfolds in a variety of formats. The number of companies implementing powerful artificial intelligence systems is still limited, but many organizations of all sizes use small solutions that require less configuration and management. To visualize the varying degrees in which companies can apply AI is based around a critical determining factor: level of involvement. This involvement includes elements within the company, such as the funds required to develop and support its artificial intelligence system, in which AI play a decisive role in your core business or daily business, and how complex your AI applications are. Firms that implement limited involvement, the AI solutions benefit from lower barriers to entry (e.g., fewer resources required) but may be unable to actualize the full potential that more robust, high involvement which AI solutions have to offer. Contrast firms implementing high involvement AI solutions can see a broad range of benefits at the core of their business because it is the analytics that has evolved to where it can handle problems that are relatively unstructured and come up with suggestions in a way that would once have been considered “expert” and even defined as AI. An important feature that distinguishes artificial intelligence from classic "advanced analytics" is the automation of feedback and improvement loops, namely learning by the system (machine learning) about how to do things better, and this, in turn, implies that conclusions are being checked and rated according to certain criteria, rather than being reviewed by the person who decides what to do next. Where the action is “managed” by AI is precise and contained, implemented quickly, and with the results also being measurable and assessable quickly, which makes it productive especially in the field of marketing. Artificial intelligence is increasingly used in operational marketing, such as identification of risks, contact center response management, as well as in marketing including analysis and targeting of customers, design, and selection of advertising copy to match target customers, pricing to maximize yield from individual customers with powered solutions provide marketers with a central platform for managing a huge amount of data, these platforms can derive insightful marketing intelligence into your target audience so you can make data-driven decisions about how to best reach out to your customers are some of the key benefits of leveraging artificial intelligence in marketing through increased campaign ROI if leveraged AI platforms can make a fast decision on how to best allocate funds across the media channels or analyze the most effective ad placements to more constantly engage customers and get more value out of the campaign. It also ensures greater customer relationships and real-time personalization and can help marketers in delivering personalized messages to their customers and can also help market us to identify customers and target them with the information that will get them to re-engage with the brand because these AI-driven algorithms process large amounts of data within minutes to provide meaningful business-base which makes the entire decision-making process easier and faster. In this way, artificial intelligence makes business decisions easier. In the present scenario, AI experts believe it's going to be one of the main drivers of the fourth Industrial Revolution and that it has the potential to not just transform the tech sectors but other sectors as well which is going to open a new chapter of the society of the world because AI is going to deliver so many improvements and the quality of our lives it is a renaissance, a golden age of machine learning and artificial intelligence that was the realm of science fiction for the last several decades. Artificial intelligence may be the most important thing ever studied in the humanities, and it is more in-depth than any work that uses technology It is important to take full advantage while minimizing shortcomings and focus on autonomous systems, such as autonomous driving systems that act as self-driving cars mother of all AI projects and has made applications like self-driving technology viable for the first time, three things happen at the same time number one data collection and data processing became easier because of better technologies right um you need data to fuel AI training and that's been one of the big drivers the second thing that has happened is that computer processing has become faster that's like the engine so no matter how much fuel you have if you don't have that engine and processing the data on a timeframe that's reasonable was just not possible and the third thing that's happened is that new algorithms have been developed which has made AI much more powerful so technology has been changing and developing at a pace that's much faster than ever before which simplifies decision making.

Role of Technology In Startups-Expectations vs Reality

We progress not only through growth but also use of more products; we also progress by preserving our environments in a very sensitive way so that is where technology plays a new role by permeating different walks of life from basic needs to the sophisticated needs and how there could be opportunities in all such technological value chains for startups to come and deliver some specific value. As many of the business processes are rendered machine led which means that technology has replaced the traditional way of conducting business processes. Due to which technology has become more omnipresent than it was ever before. It provides opportunities for companies to emerge and these opportunities and services could be seen as a black box. On one side there is a product and on the other side, we have a customer. The product is made by the entrepreneur in a particular way and then delivered to the customer. But underlying the product is a technology and overwhelming the customer is the valuation of the company. Thus, on the left side, the product and the underlying technology on the right side, we have customers or the marketplace and the overarching market valuation for the company. So, what goes on within this box of conversion called entrepreneurship is indeed a black and very specific box to each entrepreneur, specific to each context. But the goal of every entrepreneur is not only to solve a problem, not only to produce a product innovatively but also to achieve a claim and also achieve market valuation. In the United States, Fintech, E-commerce, internet software, and services lead the pack. In China, artificial intelligence leads the pack, under which China is trying to develop itself in the new industrial path. However, India is imitating the Western model with Fintech supply chain, E-commerce, auto, and transportation leading the pack, and is considered to be one of the largest ecosystems, startup ecosystems in the world numbering 7000 to 10000 startups which shows that developed industrial countries such as South Korea, Germany, Singapore, Japan and Sweden trial behind India in global unicorn club do not mean that modern technologies or futuristic technologies not being pursued by startups in those countries rather it could mean that the big companies, big industrial labs, big corporate laboratories in those countries are in the forefront of developing those kinds of technologies that is one possibility. The other possibility is that startups are indeed functioning in that area and developing those futuristic technologies which are based upon two types of innovation, one is a sustainable innovation which does not disrupt this market situation that is the customers remains as they are, the products by enlarging remains they are, but the product themselves have been substantially improved to lead to a different kind of state of the art for the market as well as for the product. The second is disruptive innovation or a product market situation, certain products fit certain markets and certain markets require certain products. This is the product market configuration that happens like automobiles requiring automobile users, coal requiring thermal power plants. Therefore, a startup that probably adopts lots of followership strategies will be high on product profitability, but probably low on innovation. On the other hand, a differentiating business or startup would be high on innovation but probably low on product profitability, but a company that achieves high innovation intensity, as well as high product profitability, may term it as a strategically outstanding company. And every company must aspire to be in that quadrant of having a high level of product innovation as well as a high level of product profitability. The example which we went through previously is the light bulb, the movement from CFL to let us say LED is sustainable innovation, the product market configuration remained the same, but the way the industry developed itself and the way the consumer started using the bulbs has substantially changed and why this is an innovation because if somebody does not follow this technological path and chooses to be in the previous generation of products that company would go away. The industry would not go away, but the company would go away. Therefore, all companies need to pursue innovation. Technology has even changed the traditional nature of customers as they earlier used to be homogenously segmented that is high-paying customers, mid-paying customers, low-paying customers, or high-quality based customers, luxury customers than developing markets customers, or middle-income customers and low-income customers. Today it is completely heterogeneous, it is layered, and is much more interconnected in the market place which changed the traditional rules of industrial development on a certain scale and expands the scope to enter a new industry based on new technology. They are being rewritten that business model is going to go out of the window in the period of digitalization because of the emerging market sensing companies and the pioneering startup system they all have a synergy that synergy works through digitization, through the deployment of science and technology, but the startup movement is something which can energize the established product-based firms in a particular manner. Which can provide certain structures, systems, and technology to the market sensing group of entrepreneurs, and by itself the pioneering leadership can create new markets completely new markets. When technological value chain results in the complete realization of technological innovation it leads to commercial success and when technological innovation and commercial success combine it leads to financial valuation. Therefore, numbers of startup firms especially in India, which have come in the logistic space, are looking at either the first-mile delivery or the last-mile delivery, digitization of leading movement, or tracking of movements under emergency conditions things like that. They are looking at one part of the overall transportation business value chain, the overall transportation technological value chain they are looking at one aspect providing technological solutions there and they are becoming successful startups. But the point is that when the startups tend to focus more on technology rather than on the business value chain it is also possible that the power of technology as it flows from design to delivery gets diluted a bit. So, startups need to look at the scope of the overall global business potential for those startup technologies sky could be the limit and therefore the startups must be cognizant of the reaching dimensions of the technological developments they are doing with their startup activities.

CHAPTER SEVEN

Important Stratergies In Finance

What is the scope will it depends upon the brand and how it makes the portfolio and there are two stages for that:-

1. First is corporate parenting which is about how the parents should add the value.
2. The second stage is about the portfolio matrices it is about how the SBU should invest in

Corporate strategic direction works in a square method in which there are two products services first is the existing Marketing Services include marketing penetration and conglomerate diversification. The second type includes market development and new product and services which falls under the ambit of new market services. In order to understand the existing Marketing Services it is important to understand what diversification is.

A Diversification involves the increasing range of products or markets served by an organization. A Related diversification involves diversifying into products or services with relationship to the existing business while the conglomerate or the unrelated diversification involves diversifying into products or services with no relationship to the existing business.

Another area of existing marketing strategy include marketing penetration which refers to the strategy of increasing share of current market with the current product range the strategy has four factors to consider in first is about strategic capabilities which is about building on establishments. The second is about the scope which is unchanged which means the organization. The third aspect includes the increase in power which leads to the greater market share and with buyers and suppliers. But the fourth and the most important factor is Economics of sale which provide greater and experiencing curve benefits however there are constraints of market penetration which includes relation from competitors and the legal constraints and it affect into the economic constraints which includes recession for funding crisis.

Consolidation and retrenchment are other important strategies.

The consolidation refers to a strategy by which an organisation focuses defensively on their current market with current products while retrenchment refers to a strategy withdrawal from marginal activities in order to concentrate on the most valuable segments and products within their existing businesses and another important strategy and the business development is product and its development with refers to a strategy by which organisation delivers modified or new products to existing markets. The product development involves wearing degree of related diversification in terms of the product it can be expensive and high risk it may require new strategic capabilities and could typically involve project management risk.

Market development strategy involves an organization which offers existing products to new Market. The strategy basically involves different degrees of related diversification in terms of the market it entails some product development for example styling and packaging it can take the form of attracting new users, for example through extending use of aluminum to the automobile industry it can even take the form of a new geographies for example extending the market covered to new areas which could be International markets being considering most important however under this strategy it is important that the market must meet the critical success factors in order to succeed it may even required new strategic capabilities especially in marketing.

Conglomerate diversification takes the organization beyond both its existing market and its existing products and radically increase the organization scope did drivers of diversification include exploiting Economics of scope efficiency gains through applying the organization to existing resources or competences to New Market or services trenching corporate management competences exploiting superior internal process and increasing market power

The portfolio matrices include growth or share Matrix also known as BCG Matrix for the directional policy Matrix and most importantly the parenting matrix the growth share BCG Matrix has four important dimensions to consider which include stars? Cash cow and Dogs which is an important factor for determining the market growth a star is a business unit which has a high market share in a growing market while a question mark or a problem child is a business unit in a growing market but it does not have a high market share a cash cow is a business unit that has the highest market share in a mature market and dog is a business unit that has a low market share in a static or declining market this plays a very important role and acts as a decisive strategy under marketing domain.

Pricing Strategy : The importance of price strategy in a business development while developing an effective price strategy it is important to considered it as a part of a marketing plan it enables company to set prices consistent with its objectives and appropriate for a targeting marketing.

Some of the important factors which affect the price include:-

Cost and expenses

Supply and demand technology

AI consumer perception

Competition government regulation

The cost and expenses include rents utilities and insurance premiums which affect price. Fixed costs and expenses are not subject to change depending on the number of units sold. A variable cost are subject to change depending on the number of units sold its basically include the cost of goods and services sales Commission delivery charges and Advertising which affect price.

Therefore if a company is selling goods their costs are affected by the pricing structure in the channel of distribution e channel member has to make a profit to make handling the goods worth while their cost and profit together is the cost.

Law of Supply and Demand in Finance

The law of supply and demand also affects price when the demand for a product is high and supply is low the companies can increase the price when the demand for a product is low and supply is high they much met or set low prices. While working with the consumer perception the price of the product should help to create an image in the minds of customer if the prices are too low customer may consider the product to be inferior and if it is too high it will turn the customer away. The competition can affect pricing when the target market is price conscious because competitors pricing and determined the pricing of a company businesses can charge higher prices than competitors if they offer added value such as personal attention credit and warranties.

Some of the government regulations which state that it is important for a company or a business to be fair to customer and families with Federal and State Law that address pricing which includes:-

Pricing gouging

Price fixing

Resale price maintenance unit Pricing bait and

Switch advertising

Apprise gorging is an illegal practices in which competing companies agree formally or informally to restrict prices within a specified range

Price fixing means pricing above the market when no other retailer is available

Resale price maintenance is fixing imposed by manufacturer or wholesale or retail resellers of a product to deter price base competition but it is illegal

Unit pricing is the pricing of goods on the basis of cost per unit of measure such as pound or an ounce in addition to the price per item

Bait and switch is descriptive method of selling in which a customer attracted to a store bi sale price item is told either that the advertise item is unavailable or that it is inferior to a higher price item which is available this practice are not illegal but are unfair to a customer in the marketing domain. The upcoming Technology trends in the field of Internet affect the price strategy adapting to technological changes can give an entrepreneur a competitive edge not adopting can cause some businesses to become absolute

Some of the emerging Technology cal Trends are based upon setting prices and their objective include:-

1. Obtaining a target return on investment
2. Obtaining market share social and ethical concerns
3. Meeting the competition price

4. Establishing in image survival
5. Maintaining status quo

The pricing strategy decisions is based upon a target market first is to select a basic approach to pricing then determine the pricing policy following by setting a price based on the stage of the product life cycle. While setting a base price there are three basic approaches to pricing first is cost based pricing followed by demand based pricing and at the last competition based pricing

Some of the important pricing policies which a business should cater to includes establishing a pricing policy frees you from making the same pricing decision over and over again and let employees and customer know what to expect. A flexible price policy is one in which customer pay different prices for the same type for amount of merchandise. A one price policy is one in which all the customer are charged the same price for all the goods and services offered for sale. The product life cycle pricing moves through a four stage life cycle which includes an introduction growth maturity and finally a decline.

Price skimming is a process which is commonly used when the product is introduced the practice is based upon charging a higher price on a new product or service in order to recover cost and maximize profits as quickly as possible the prices then dropped when the product or service is no longer unique on the other hand the penetration pricing is also commonly used when product is introduced it is a method used to build sales by charging a low initial price to keep unit cost to customer as low as possible

The psychology of pricing techniques it includes:-

Prestige pricing odd-even pricing bundle pricing

Price lining

Multiple unit pricings

Promotion AI pricing

A business may use Prestige pricing to Foster a high and image Prestige pricing is a technique in which higher than average prices are used to suggest the status and Prestige to the customer. When a business uses odd even pricing customers may think they are getting a bargain it is a technique in which odd numbered prices are used to suggest bargain such as rupees 199 instead of 200 rupees. Price lining is a technique in which items in a certain quality category are price the same for example a store which sells a jeans at 600 800 and 1000 rupees. A promotional pricing technique is a one in which floor prices are offered for a limited period of time to stimulate sales for example a new restaurant that offer a 1990 prices for three day only in using a promotional strategy. It is important to understand how it works and what are the different types of pricing strategies which could help to change a or developing a business. However it is important to understand the possible changes which can bring in under the pricing strategies it includes adjusting the prices to maximize profit reacting to market prices revising terms of sales

Adjusting prices to maximize profit include whether the product prices are elastic or inelastic or whether the prices of the competitor are more or less, reacting to market prices is about the ongoing market research which keeps an eye on current market prices for the products if competitive prices fall then there is a chance that your company might lose customers if you do not lower the prices and the competitive prices rise it is an important for the business financial health to raise prices. Another way to change the pricing strategy is to revise the terms of sale which includes:-

1) Changing credit policies

2) Introducing discounts

3) Offering leases

4) Arranging financing

It is also important to understand the framework of The E-Commerce payment method which includes a debit card which is issued by a financial institution which can be used as an alternative to cash purchase amount on debit card or withdrawn directly from the Purchase checking or savings account.

E- Cash is a legal form of electronic money transfer used in e-commerce and transacted via the internet.

E-wallet is a software application that store the customer data such as name address and credit card number for easy retrieval during online purchase

Merchant account is a bank account that enables a business to receive that proceed of credit card purchases.

Return on investment (ROI) is the amount earned as a result of an investment.

Selling price is the actual or projected price per unit.

Smart card is an electronic prepaid cash card that includes a computer chip which can store data and is used to make purchases of financial transactions over the internet.

Consumer Satisfaction, value and retention

Customer perceived value (CPV) : The difference between the prospective customer‘s evaluation of all benefits and all the cost of an offering and the perceived alternatives.

Customer perceived value (CPV) = Total Customer Value (TCV)- Total Customer

Cost (TCC)

Total Customer Value: the perceived monetary value of the bundle of economic,

Functional and psychological benefits customer expect from a given market offering.

Total Customer Cost: the bundle of costs customers expect to incur in evaluating

Steps in a Customer Value Analysis

1. Identify major attributes and benefits that customers value
2. Assess the qualitative importance of different attributes and benefits
3. Assess the company's and competitor's performances on the different customer values against rated importance.
4. Examine ratings of specific segments
5. Monitor customer values over time

Quality V/s Loyalty

Quality is the totality of features and characteristics of a product or service that bear on its ability to satisfy stated or implied needs.

Customer Perception- Easier to maintain once established. As long as the product quality and the level of service provided to the customer remain the same, brand-loyal customers will feel little need to check out the competition.

Loyalty is a deeply held commitment to re-buy or re-patronize a preferred product or service in the future despite situational influences and marketing efforts having the potential to cause switching behavior.

Customer Spending- Maintained through the overall low prices and offering regular loyalty discounts, special offers, or multi-buy deals.

Retailing: Omni-Channel Strategy

It is our General perception that Clothes been purchased more Online than offline this days in Digital World But in US, still 87-88 per cent still is physical. China, 82 per cent is still physical. Physical is still larger. The only thing- IN-store retailing has over online Shopping ,Online doesn't have ,its ability to touch,smell, feel, and experience which offline Stores Provide. Most online companies gained prominence since 2014 when the battle among Flipkart, Snapdeal and Amazon was intense. As a result, consumers went online and tried to monetise the deep discounts available.

However, with deep discounts coming off, online transactions started Falling. Omni channel strategy Indian Retailers success mantra: Right Blend of Online + Offline. Post bitterly fought wars between brick and mortar stores (Offline Sores) and e commerce companies (Online Stores), players offering a complete and seamless consumer experience. Hence, online retailers are shifting offline (Look at Amazon s tie up with Shoppers Stop ,Marriage of Online & Offline Player), we anticipate offline stores will start moving to the digital medium to target consumers (Take example of Future Retail shifting to Retail 3.0). Omni channel strategy is the way ahead (Offline + Online Business). Among categories in Retail Industry, Food &Groceries , electronics and low value jewellery are most likely to get push on Online platform due to High Standardization, While Apparels due to Low Standardization still preferred to be offline platform

Purchase Branded apparels deploy omni channel strategy with online as well as offline presence.

Retail 3.0 , Omni Channel Strategy : Blend of online and offline Globally, 2.5bn plus consumers are connected to the internet. In India, ~400mn consumers are connected to internet, of which ~300mn are smartphone users. These consumers, on an average, spend ~3 hours a day on the internet. By 2020, India is expected to have 700mn (300mn English users, 200mn Hindi users and 200mn other languages) internet users with 700mn smartphone users consuming 10GB of data. Thus, digital is a bridge between the consumers and sellers. Using this bridge, online can drive offline business as consumers will use best of both the platforms. Hence, companies can blend the best of both the platforms to provide seamless experience to consumers. offline channel offer consumer experience the brand (touch, smell, visible senses) while digital enhances only visible senses but provides assortments and convenience. However, going ahead, online and offline channels will be blended to provide seamless experience to consumers. Digital can provide deep understanding of consumer behaviour using data analytics and will be used to personalise targeting.

Online penetration differs across categories: Food & Groceries V/s Apparels. High Standardization V/s Low Standardization Products E commerce spurt prompted Brick & Morter stores to revisit their strategies. They realised that certain categories were impacted more by e commerce. But they also realised that consumers preferred to see, touch and feel the product before purchasing it. For instance,electronics focused formats and home focused stores came under heavy pressure. The initial market share loss was due to heavy discounting. However online will not affect high value jewellery (intricate designs). categories like electronics and low value jewellery may see a shift to e commerce channel,Online due to High Standardization nature of Product. Branded apparels will pursue omni channel strategy and be present in online as well as offline channels. Indian Retail Apparels & Clothes are Net gainers in PHYGITAL Era : B&M retailers are investing heavily in apparels as margins are higher compared to other categories; margins in private labels can go up to 60% (current 40%). However, with the birth of the e commerce industry, B&M retailers are feeling the pinch. Consumers select (trial & fit) clothes and shoes from B&M retailers, but order them online at a much cheaper price (e commerce companies are pricing products at huge discounts). However, now, with deep discounts off the table, in our view, B&M retailers will do better. Further, most of these retailers are implementing omni channel strategies. Consumers can order online and then go to the store to check the fit and then accept the product. These initiatives will help B&M retailers make a comeback after losing market share to e commerce companies.

To be relevant and accessible, physical stores are needed. Thus, Lenskart has 350 stores in ~90 cities (both tier 1 and 2). online beauty brands retailer Nykaa. It already has

8 stores in Delhi NCR, Mumbai, Bengaluru, Amritsar and Pune under the Luxe and On Trend categories.

The Luxe stores will mostly have luxury and premium brands. Oppo is planning to open own stores, Chinese smart phone maker to sell directly to consumers and add to its existing wholesale business. The move will help Oppo expand its reach in the world's 2nd largest smartphone market. Walmart-Flipkart deal: Amplify Domestic retail Boom One of the largest and much anticipated deal has been finally sealed. Walmart has acquired ~77% stake in Flipkart for ~USD16bn, including USD2bn of primary infusion.

How is the Walmart-Flipkart deal lead to change the domestic retail industry s dynamics?

(i) online & offline partnerships are likely to get a Boost;

(ii) online discounting may not necessarily increase (as Walmart may drive private labels/Their own in house product rather than focus only on other branded product); and

(iii) FMCG companies are likely to benefit as Walmart s expertise lies in hypermarkets/grocery retailing (plans to tie up with kirana players).

(iv) Also, subject to regulations, there is likelihood of Walmart s cash & carry business being integrated with Flipkart at some point in time an added kicker. 1How will sector dynamics change? India s organised retail is set for a fortunate twist. The e-commerce boom had seen emergence of many players. However, cut throat competition had led to many of them eventually shutting shop. But, the ones who weathered the storm Flipkart, Amazon and Alibaba backed PayTM have emerged stronger. This shows that, all large physical retailers are moving towards the omni-channel. Hence, the probable threat, if any, from these online platforms will also be limited. Also, considering that organised retail constitutes only 10% of the overall retail pie, there is enough room for all the players to grow. We also believe, global retail giants could look at large physical retailers as attractive JV/ acquisition candidates for their India entry.

Triple Bottom Line in Business strategey

TBL Framework helps to achieve the goal of the sustainability of business practices that examine profits to include environmental and social issues to measure the total cost of cases. After the release of the Brundtland report in 1987, the term sustainable development was unwise and CSR also gained popularity. The TBL came as an expression of the new language to expand the inevitable expansion of environmental protection till that time sustainability was majorly focused on environmental protection only businesses focused on economic aspects only considering sustainability as a counteractive force for economic justice as the sustainable development can only be possible if social and ecological elements were also considered essential to the business along with economic adamant and the language needed to be able to resonate with businesses and corporates. The term TBL was used forcefully in an article in the California management review on business strategies by Elkington in 1994. The triple bottom line of 21st century looks at three essential elements that are the three P's:-

People is about socially responsible operations

Planet It's about environmental conservation and conservation

Profit It's about business profit and loss

The TBL is a combination of corporate social responsibility (CSR) and environmental impact assessment (EWA) and the traditional bottom. There are seven major drivers of the TBL agenda also called revolutions that occurred in sustainability. These are forced the market to shift from a bare compliance mindset to a competition mindset as they sense the business opportunity changed with the worldwide shift in social and human values forced the businesses to rethink their usual business. Transparency has become a distinguishing factor for industries now more open companies are thought to be reliable and trustworthy fourth lifecycle technology now companies are required to think about the complete lifecycle of the product from cradle to grave or even cradle to cradle go on are the days of consideration of product at the point of selling only it's essential to know functional aspects as well how it has met how it has shipped and what to become of it after its useful life. Thus, these partnerships instead of competing unnecessarily many companies are finding that it's beneficial to form a partnership.

The application of the Triple Bottom line in a business can be understood through case study of plant cell: The Plant cells belong to the circle environment of the final triple. If these plant cells are the original designers of the structure, it is the circle on which everything depends or where everything is incorporated. Everything comes from nature at some point. Society, which is related to the social circle of the triple bottom line, exists within the environment, and the economy is a byproduct of society.

So, instead of three overlapping circles, there are three interlocking circles where the economy is a wholly controlled subsidiary of the environment. To achieve sustainability, we must respect social and environmental conditions: satisfying human needs within the limits of ecological constraints.

Economic decisions are part of a strategy to make more money by moving closer to social and ecological sustainability. The economy is a means to an end, not the end itself. It's important to remember that paying the bills happens on multiple levels and ultimately we're all dependent on photosynthesis. This is helpful for businesses because it provides a new perspective on the rationale for integrating sustainability into who and how they are in the world. Due to the advancement of IT long-term thinking is essential for sustainability. The corporate governance has to be inclusive to many stakeholders the sole focus on the shareholder will make the business unsustainable in the long term proper balance should be achieved between shareholders and stakeholders. There are implementation phase features of TBL strategies which include:-

1) Socially responsible operation- It establishes that the company should take responsibility for social and environmental issues arising from its operations

2) Conversions improvements in social aspects will invariably improve economic profitability as well

3) Novelty promise the novelty promise offered by TBL is questionable for measurement claims it's not clear how to measure the social and environmental bottom line

4) Transparency promise and reliability claims company will be transparent with all stakeholders but can internal reporting team report actual operations the actual damage and wrong deeds is questioned.

Conclusion:-

Therefore, simultaneous working is essential but it is difficult for businesses to balance all three elements simultaneously because the current pattern of wealth creation is continuously worsening environmental and social problems therefore the pressure would increase continuously on governments and corporations to improve their operations and make a transition to sustainable development.

The TBL performance and PPL gave rise to many sustainability agendas and it provoke deeper thinking about capitalism and its future but people in the early time of its inception only got construed it as a balancing tool with a trade-off mentality this won't solve the cultural hardwired problems related to business thinking while following TBL the importance given to prophets element is higher and people and planet are ignored also while decision-making decisions made through prophets perspective seldom contribute to people and planet positively. Many experts have expressed that at a minimum, one may have progressed in two dimensions while the third remains unchanged, so companies have to work around the deployment of the concept and truly essential requirements of social and environmental elements to ensure the efficiency of Triple Bottom Line in Business.

CHAPTER EIGHT

Importance of Consumer Behavior

In the marketing domain, a behavior that consumer displays in searching, evaluating, purchasing, and disposing of products that they think will satisfy their needs or those acts of individuals directly involved in obtaining and using economic goods and services including the decision process that precedes and determine their acts refer to as consumer behavior. Marketers have understood the importance of the process of stimulus generalization that has become critical to branding and packaging solutions that try to combine active consumer associations with existing brand or company names. Marketers can develop some strategies based on general incentives. Family brands enable products to take advantage of the reputation of the company name. Marketers can expand the product line by adding related products to existing brands. The consumers can detect the difference between these different stimuli is relative. Exposure occurs when the stimulus is within the range of human sensory receptors. However, Consumers concentrate on some stimuli but are unaware of others. Under consumer behavior, psychophysics represents the science of how the physical environment fits into our subjective world. Advertising can use consumer self-esteem to promote products by offering products as a way to treat low self-esteem. Self-esteem promotional materials are a way to treat low self-esteem. Self-concept strongly influences our behavior as consumers and these products can play a pivotal role in defining our self-concept. Society's expectations of masculinity and femininity determine the products we buy and the products we try to meet expectations. The way we view our bodies is an integral part of our self-esteem.

Every culture has norms for beauty which will influence how we view our bodies and decorate ourselves consumers make decisions they are influenced by the situation which led to instrumental conditioning which occurs in three ways, positive reinforcements, negative reinforcements, and punishments. Positive reinforcement enters the form of a reward. Negative reinforcement shows how a negative outcome can be prevented. When an unpleasant event occurs after the reaction, punishment occurs. Absorption occurs when there is no gain or reinforcement. In other words, the conditioning is inactivated because it is not reinforced. Instrumental conditioning (or operant conditioning) occurs when we learn to perform behavior's that produce favorable outcomes and prevent those that yield negative outcomes. Although classical conditioning is involuntary and quite simple, instrumental conditioning is consciously created to achieve goals. The desired behavior over a while as a shaping process rewards our intermediate actions. Instrumental conditioning occurs in one of three ways Positive reinforcement comes in the form of a reward. Negative reinforcement shows how a negative outcome can be avoided, third is a punishment which occurs when unpleasant events follow a response. In other words, regulation is inactivated because it is not encouraged. Marketers need to determine the most effective reinforcement plan because the decision is related to the quantity of effort and resources they put in to reward consumers who adequately meet their needs. Several schedules are possible. In fixed interval reinforcement, the first response made promises the reward, and then on a specific set interval, future rewards are given. With variable interval reinforcement, one doesn't know when the reward will be offered or when to expect the reinforcement; consumers have to respond at a consistent rate. Marketers can use the characteristics that explain conformity to persuade individuals to follow consumer trends. Depending on the solution in question, the choice may include some or all of the group members, and different group members may play different roles, the initiator role is played by the person who brings up the idea or identifies the need. The person who searches for information in the group and controls the flow of information is the gatekeeper. The person who tries to influence the outcome of the decision is the influential person. The person who makes the purchase is the buyer. Those who will use the product are the users. Organization buyers are affected by a variety of factors, including the psychological characteristics of the makers involved in the purchase decision and external stimuli, such as the nature of the industry and the organization, cultural factors, and the level of risk and complexity involved in the decision. The level of complexity depends upon the level of information the buyer must gather before the decision, the seriousness of the decisions and reviews of alternatives, and the buyer's familiarity with the type of purchase.

Three basic types of decisions are straight rebuy, modified rebuy, and new task. Direct purchase or straight rebuy offer a standard solution. The revised repurchase or modified rebuy involves limited decision-making. The new task involves manifold problems, to be solved because the company has not yet made a similar decision. For example, the Coca-Cola bottle also illustrates an example of how design can facilitate product success. Consumer senses play a significant role in the decisions marketers make. For example, marketers rely completely on visual elements in advertising and packaging. They convey meaning in visual channels through the color, size, and style of the product. For example, some brands utilize scents easily. These aspects are referred to as the brand's sensory system. Many of our reactions to colors are based on establishing associations. These are cultural connotations like the color black for mourning. But other reactions are biological. Because colors are so powerful, they pose a major challenge to packaging design. Ultimately, they can become part of the company's business image or trademark. Therefore, these different aspects of consumer behavior play a significant role in the field of marketing.

AI and Automation in Marketing: Views from Customer's Perspective

Marketing currently represents the 4th largest use of AI concerning resources spent, and the 5th largest industry adopter of AI technology, with around 2.50% of the total industry. Under Artificial Intelligence, computer technologies hold a vital role in helping businesses to connect with their customers as it comes with powerful reporting tools that enable them to gain better insights into customer behavior. All these are presented through an intuitive screen.

By gaining powerful customer insights marketers can make fast decisions while optimizing their digital campaigns that target the right audience and helps marketers to make informed decisions through data analysis, natural language processing media buying automated decision making content generation, or real-time personalization's through its key components like machine learning, big data, and analytics the platform AI also provides increased speed of decision-making, especially in response to new data being available or competitive threats emerging, allowing companies to capture the benefits of stronger market positions earlier. These benefits include-

1) Identification of missing data,

2) Increased rationality, particularly via removal or reduction of cognitive bias by decision-makers,

3) Creation of a standard basis for decision-making

4) Incorporation of learning from experience, and Higher quality management of marketing projects.

However, With AI technology being more feasible to implement than ever before, we are beginning to see its marketing potential unfolds in a variety of formats. The number of companies implementing powerful artificial intelligence systems is still limited, but many organizations of all sizes use small solutions that require less configuration and management. To visualize the varying degrees in which companies can apply AI is based around a critical determining factor: level of involvement. This involvement includes elements within the company, such as the funds required to develop and support its artificial intelligence system, in which AI play a decisive role in your core business or daily business, and how complex your AI applications are the firms that implement limited involvement, the AI solutions benefit from lower barriers to entry (e.g., fewer resources required) but may be unable to actualize the full potential that more robust, high involvement which AI solutions have to offer. Contrast firms implementing high involvement AI solutions can see a broad range of benefits at the core of their business because it is the analytics that has evolved to where it can handle problems that are relatively unstructured and come up with suggestions in a way that would once have been considered “expert” and even defined as AI.

An important feature that distinguishes artificial intelligence from classic "advanced analytics" is the automation of feedback and improvement loops, namely learning by the system (machine learning) about how to do things better, and this, in turn, implies that conclusions are being checked and rated according to certain criteria, rather than being reviewed by the person who decides what to do next. Where the action is “managed” by AI is precise and contained, implemented quickly, and with the results also being measurable and assessable quickly, which makes it productive especially in the field of marketing. Artificial intelligence is increasingly used in operational marketing, such as identification of risks, contact center response management, as well as in marketing including analysis and targeting of customers, design, and selection of advertising copy to match target customers, pricing to maximize yield from individual customers with powered solutions provide marketers with a central platform for managing a huge amount of data, these platforms can derive insightful marketing intelligence into your target audience so you can make data-driven decisions about how to best reach out to your customers are some of the key benefits of leveraging artificial intelligence in marketing through increased campaign ROI if leveraged AI platforms can make a fast decision on how to best allocate funds across the media channels or analyze the most effective ad placements to more constantly engage customers and get more value out of the campaign. It also ensures greater customer relationships and real-time personalization and can help marketers in delivering personalized messages to their customers and can also help market us to identify customers and target them with the information that will get them to re-engage with the brand because these AI-driven algorithms process large amounts of data within minutes to provide meaningful business-base which makes the entire decision-making process easier and faster.

In the present scenario, AI experts believe it's going to be one of the main drivers of the fourth Industrial Revolution and that it has the potential to not just transform the tech sectors but other sectors as well which is going to open a new chapter of the society of the world because AI is going to deliver so many improvements and the quality of our lives it is a renaissance, a golden age of machine learning and artificial intelligence that was the realm of science fiction for the last several decades. Artificial intelligence may be the most important thing ever studied in the humanities, and it is more in-depth than any work that uses technology It is important to take full advantage while minimizing shortcomings and focus on autonomous systems, such as autonomous driving systems that act as self-driving cars mother of all AI projects and has made applications like self-driving technology viable for the first time, three things happen at the same time number one data collection and data processing became easier because of better technologies right um you need data to fuel AI training and that's been one of the big drivers the second thing that has happened is that computer processing has become faster that's like the engine so no matter how much fuel you have if you don't have that engine and processing the data on a timeframe that's reasonable was just not possible and the third thing that's happened is that new algorithms have been developed which has made AI much more powerful.

Therefore, technology has been changing and developing at a pace that's much faster than ever before which simplifies decision making. In this way, artificial intelligence makes marketing easy from a consumer perspective.

Does the customer will always buy the product which delivering the greater customer value?

Not under every situation because the customer also examines his total cost of transacting with the product and the alternative, which consists of more than the money before making the buying decision. Therefore, there are three ways to making success in selling to the buyer:-

1. Increasing total customer value by improving product, services, personnel, and/or image benefits.

2. Reducing the buyer's non monetary cost by reducing the time, energy, and psychic cost.

3. Reducing its product monetary cost to the buyer.

Total Customer Satisfaction is depend on the offer's performance in relation to the customer's expectation.

Satisfaction: A person's feeling of pleasure or dissappoinment resulting from comparing a product's perceived performance (outcome) in relation to his or her expectations.

Customer Expectations

1. How do customer form their expectations?
2. From past buying experience, friend's and associates's advice, and marketer's and competitior's information and promises
3. If marketers raise expectations too high, the buyer is likely to be disappointed
4. If marketers set expectations too low, the buyer won't attract the company's offering.

In a hypercompetitive economy a company can only win the competition by creating and delivering superior values.

This involves 5 capabilities:-

1. Understanding customer value

2. Creating customer value

3. Delivering customer value

4. Capturing customer value

5. Sustaining customer value

To succeed, a company needs to use the concepts of a value chain and a value delivery network. Every firm is a synthesis of activities that are performed to design, produce, market, delivery and support its products. The value chain identifies nine strategically relevant activities that create value and cost in a specific business. These value creating activities consists of five primary activities and four support activities. The primary activities represent the sequence of bringing materials into the business (inbound logistics), converting them into final products (operations), and shipping out final.

The support activities: procurement, technology, human resource management, and firm infrastructure are handled in certain specialized departments, but not only there. For example: several departments may do some procurements and hiring of people. The firm task is to examine its cost and performance in each value creating activity and to look for ways to improve it. The firm should estimate its competitors cost and performance as benchmarks against which to compare its owns cost and performances. The firm success depends not only on how well each departments performs its works, but also on how well the various departmental activities are coordinated. Too often, company departments act to maximize their interests. To be succesful a firm also needs to look for competitive advantages beyond its own operations, into value chains of its supliers, distributors and customers. Many companies today have partnered with specific suppliers and distributors to create a superior value delivery network (supply chain)

Forming strong customer involves:-

1. Get cross-departmental participation in planning and managing the customer satisfaction and retention process.

2. Integrate the voice of customers in all business decisions.

3. Organize and make accessible a database of information on individual customer needs, preferences, contacts, purchase frequency and satisfaction.

4. Make it easy for customers to reach appropriate company personnel and express their needs, perceptions, and complaints.

5. Run award programs recognizing outstanding employee

Geofencing: The future of Targeted Marketing

In this rapidly changing world of technology, the geofencing market is projected to show major growth prospects during the forecast period. Major factor driving the geofencing market is the increasing adoption of location-based application services which is changing the way you reach your customers with the abundance of smartphones with GPS technology geofencing is the most accurate way to target mobile users where they go in the real world simply put business nucleus uses the latitude and longitude coordinates of mobile devices to show them display ads most geo-targeting technologies to target users immediately when they enter the shape and up to 30 days after they've left and any time in between use geofencing to target customers who have been to or are near your location with special offers loyalty rewards and other incentives use geofencing to target locations where your customers spend their time use geofencing to target users who are visiting your competition the possibilities are endless with geofencing powered by business nucleus geofencing is a new marketing technology that's innovative timely and can put your organization or business right in front of potential customers, thus the rise in growth of competitive analysis is another major factor responsible for fueling the growth of geofencing market.

The global geofencing market, by geography, has been segmented into North America, Europe, Asia Pacific, and the Rest of the World. As compared to other regions, the geofencing market in North America is expected to witness significant growth and hold the global market share during the forecast period. U.S. and Canada are anticipated to drive the growth of the geofencing market. This is owing to the presence of a considerable number of established key players like Apple in that region. In addition to this, the region also maintains a well-established infrastructure which allows higher penetration of devices and ultimately provides better connectivity. The increasing adoption of smartphones and the burgeoning popularity of social media platforms are expected to be another major factor responsible for driving the growth of the geofencing market. The main question how geofencing meet the targeted goal is through its application of displaying advertisements on smartphones to your potential customers and enter a particular geographic area and permeates just like a fence customers enter your specified area and suddenly your ads are appearing at just the right time the ads draw attention at the prime time when your target customers are nearest to your location or as a customer walks into an area within your store when someone uses their smartphones to search the web and you're utilizing geofence advertising your ad could appear on that device at the same time this is a great way to maximize your return on investment ROI because your ads are only seen by people who are interested in your product or service and close to your location benefits of geofence advertising your company receives many benefits from this type of marketing in addition to putting you on the leading edge of modern technology customized ads your ads are targeted to reach only people who are in your area and likely to become your new customers affordable you can start with a small campaign and enlarge it as needed by extending your fence range targeted your marketing budget is not wasted on reaching people who are not likely to become customers you can use geofence ads to reach local area people and bring them into your store and while in the store mark it to them brand awareness is increased people will become better aware of what your organization offers.

Therefore, the future is promising for geo-targeted or geofencing ads the most successful geo-targeted ads messages are customized for that user at that time that place because of its features which make it easier to reach customers and allow you to reach customers at the right place and right time. By enhancing local sales, Increase engagement and helps in creating brand awareness which enables targeted ad revenue to represent 45% of all mobile ad revenues by the year 2022. In the current scenario, marketers recognize the power of geofencing and have used it to obstruct traffic to competitors garner e-commerce transactions using detailed local demographics, and drive foot traffic to events according to a 2019 report; the increased number of mobile computing devices along with the impending integration of location-based search with social networking will be behind the massive shift for words location-based advertising in the 2021-2024 time period through geofencing.

Thus, Geofencing plays a vital role in the future of targeted marketing.

Vendor Market Strategy

Vendor management refers to the process that helps the organization's to find the winders evaluate them and ensure that they're qualified conducting business with the vendors the process is only starts once the need arises to outsource a given task pre-rendered organizations perform the following activities to accomplish vendor management researching vendors who can perform the required tasks negotiating and enter into a contract praise quotation performance evaluation preparation and maintenance of the vendor related documents processing of the payments the organization's research and come up with a list of vendors who can perform the tasks and deliver it with quality all the chosen winners are then evaluated based on the following factors capability pricing quality Pass history or goodwill initially quotations are obtained from each of the vendors their references are checked and then the company researches thoroughly through online resources once this is done their financial stability certifications and insurance details are evaluated once a list of winners are chosen the responsibility of the window manager lies in managing a list of vendors allocating tasks or contracts when necessary keep it check on their performance ensure that the grade upon contract rules are followed big organizations is really how a pool of depending on the past performance a specific vendor might be best suited for a specific task while secondary preference is given to other vendors when the preferred vendor is not able to take up a project or task are unable to deliver then the other vendors will be allocated with the assignment when our management usually requires huge documentation work the databases need to be integrated with various accounts payable systems in this process it easily requires obtaining vendor information like contact information incidents are tax related documents etc when the vendors have access to confidential information it is essential to get the non-disclosure agreement or similar agreement signed in from them and documented all such documents thus procured should be updated each year that covers the vendor management.

The quality of the input material or the service going playing a crucial role because at the end of the day we have to do a value addition on the input material or input service that we have done when we are going to do a filtering of various input materials.

If we are going to do then that means there will be a lot of productivity issues that we are going to face supplier identification can be done through a market survey and then we can have an initial visit we can do a system audit at that particular supplier and then also we can do a process audit so if we are having a confidence or both the complete or process in the system of this particular supplier including the attitude and their leadership everything we can go ahead with a further introduction and other steps that we can go through in our company as for the company procedures so once we introduce a supplier then we have to give a component to him and that we call it as a component introduction and in that we have to take care of certain specifics like advanced product quality planning from the supplier point of view and also production part approval process of this particular child parts start of production and also safe launch concept so all these things when we are having in agreement with our supplier components then even we can agree with our customers.

When we talk about the timeline we have to capture this from our customer and then have some kind of buffer and then we need to give to even suppliers also so when we fall all the things in the supply chain management then we can have a very smooth component introduction process finally we can really meet the customer agreed timeline and also the quality requirements when we talk about supplier performance it varies from you know cost quality and also the delivery so we have to balance all these three things we cannot compromise any of these three things because if you maintain the quality in the long term you get a lot of business and you will be also having very less stress because of reduced customer complaints when we talk about the delivery like how effective and how efficient how quicker you are going to do your customer will be of course happy and is going to give you a lot of many projects over a period of time cost also consistently you have to either maintain or you have to decrease and it should not be the other way around because no customer we really like when you go to them and ask for a price increase and which cn lead to disruptions, because these changes can come from an external source some of the changes can come from an internal source itself so when some of changes can be purely from certain specific supplier management issues. so we have to understand all these things and take proper corrective actions based on that so it can be a price increase which our supplier is asking we need to understand why exactly is asking like that and then it can be the poor quality or if it is only a one batch then you can always take some kind of corrective action and then go ahead an improvement but if there is a recurring complaint with respect to the similar parts or similar defects then we have to take that very seriously and delay delivery also creates a lot of disruption in our supply chain our production line may stop and our customer line may stop at the end of the day they are going to penalize us and we have to transfer that particular penalty to our complete supply chain we have to consider all these aspects so that's why we need to have a prop escalation management process in handling these kind of issues so to conclude we understood the importance of vented management how it plays a very important role in maintaining the input quality and not only maintaining that we need to also sustain that over a period of time with the help of a process called as escalation management.

CHAPTER NINE

Human Resources

HR is the pattern of planned, emerging human resource strategies intended to enable an organization and its goal while simultaneously reproducing the HR base, over a long-lasting calendar year, and controlling for self-induced side, and feedback effects, on the HR systems, the HR base, and thus on the company itself.

To ensure sustainability, HR assumes, that an organization is an open system, that needs to develop and regenerate, its human resources at least, as far as, it consumes them, and this is linked to the paradoxes. Sustainable HR also assumes that employees are constantly replenishing and using. There is a need to have, sustainable human resource management systems. Because, human beings are the primary resource, that organizations have.

The most important goal is to sustain develop and reproduce, an organization's human, and social resource base which includes:-

- The mutual exchange relationships
- Ensuring the output-input ratio, over a long period
- To evaluate and assess the negative effects of human resource activities, on the human resource base, and the

sources for human resources.

- Keeping the inflow, in balance with the outflow. Keeping people, motivated enough, so that their productivity, and getting them to be, as productive as possible

These balances need to be achieved, through interpretations of sustainability which can be normative, efficiency-related, or substance-related. Normative relates to, what should be done. Efficiency relates to the productivity and substance material, which is the tangibility of the situation.

There are some organizational effects of efficiency which includes:-

Sustained competitive advantages

Innovativeness

Productivity

If employees are being productive and their efficiency is high, then the competitive advantage will be maintained. There are some important aspects of sustainability of HR which includes:-

Social effects: The normative interpretations of sustainability are social legitimacy, accountability to the stakeholders, accountability to anyone, who has put efforts into trust, trustworthiness, quality of life, good relations.

Ecological effects: The usage of the location of work, results in the reduction of costs, travel for work, etc. This is in turn affected by, results in green products, services, and volunteer programs. All of this, is in turn, happening in an organizational context that is feeding into the source of HR origin.

Perception of consistency among decision-makers: The policies need to be, made by, different people who will be contributing, to the formulation of different policies, at different stages.

Support from the management: defining the policies, and implementing the policies, is critical to the success of, sustainable human resources management.

Therefore, these factors influence the formulation and implementation of the HR policies, to help the HR function, become more sustainable, are appropriate, in the context of economic, social, and ecological, outcomes. Whatever companies are doing, needs to be appropriate, needs to be tailored, needs to fit into the context of, the economic, social, and ecological, outcomes of whatever it is, that you do. Relevance to, the current needs, future needs, future anticipated needs of the employees is important in incorporating sustainable HR practices.

Digital Transformation in the Human Resources Domain

We sleep in a world where everyone seems to be perpetually connected. we tend to square measure unconsciously manufacturing a pair of.4 Quintillion bytes of knowledge day after day. Over the last 2 years, alone 90% of the information within the world was generated. This trend affects, however, we tend to communicate and the way we tend to consume info, however additionally however businesses operate. Seventy-six of corporations believe huge information is probably going to essentially amendment their operations over consequent 2 years. An hour is not any exception.

In 2019 alone simple fraction of the CEOs across the world enforced a minimum of one or a lot of those technologies into the approach that they are doing business. And these embrace computing, thus this is often once more swing something informed the cloud. concerning five-hundredths of IT, organizations have place concerning 1/2 what accustomed be in server rooms out into the cloud, and it permits them to quite a pivot and adapt and befits new technologies approaching and relinquishing of a number of that risk. And then, robotic method automation and this is often any physical task and having the ability to quite automotive those easy tasks and want to rely on what upskill has to happen within the organization as a result of that hour digital transformation is that the method of fixing operational hour processes to become machine-driven and data-driven. In step with the 2018 Human Capital Trends report, they place it this manner. It's concerning hour groups creating up the twin challenge of remodeling hour operations on the one hand and reworking the hands and also the approach work is completed on the opposite. In different words, instead of hour digital transformation is simply concerning hour, it is a metamorphosis that involves organizations as an entire. Naturally, digital transformation does not happen long. Organizations do not go from being barely digital to being digital within the blink of an eye fixed. Trendy hour systems believe over ever on automation, analytics, and prophetical capabilities exploitation hands information allows hour to create choices that drive each higher business, and other people outcomes. Now, you are most likely thinking: this is often all abstract. Our company's implementing hour Associate in Nursingalytics? the solution is an absolute yes! And you recognize them too. Multinationals like Facebook, Amazon Credit Suisse, Google, and LinkedIn square measure all doing it. Credit Suisse saves up to 100 million bucks once a year, by increasing the retention rate when making a lot of data-driven hours operate. Big data, huge savings. Corporations that implement individuals analytics square measure fifty-six a lot of profitable than their less data-driven competitors.

That's why, within the last decade, seventy-two of companies within the United States hyperbolic their defrayal on analytics. And a lot of investments result in a lot of jobs. The digital hand analytics market is predicted to be valued at over one billion bucks by the year 2024. There are six stages of digital transformation -One, business as was common. this does not need any clarification. Two; gift and active. Varied experiments through the organizations drive digital acquisition and creative thinking. Three, formalize. This is often wherever the business connection comes in. If the Associate in the Nursing experiment is not relevant for the business, leadership should not support it. Four, people begin to understand the ability to collaborate. Their shared efforts and insights result in new strategic road maps. 5 converged. a fervent digital transformation team is made to guide the company's strategy and operations. Six; innovative and adjustable.

Digital transformation has become the new business as was common and a replacement system is established. All right, currently, we all know what method we're talking about;

let's take a glance at that factors square measure necessary for a thriving digital transformation.

One; as a rule of thumb, any hour transformation, whether or not it is a digital one or not, has got to happen with a transparent objective in mind. it's to create business sense.

Two; you wish to create absolute to get all stakeholders from workers to the C suite and everybody in between is on board.

Three; do not overcomplicate things. This suggests beginning easy and little. Consider the areas of your hour processes that would do with a digital makeover.

Four; rank ideas can most likely lead to a protracted list of ideas. Rank they supported impact and energy. Begin with the ideas that square measure high impact and low effort.

Fifth; critically assess what works and what does not.

Six; culture is very important. A digital attitude among the whole hands from the new individuals you rent via your current workers is important for a thriving transformation. The projected quantity of jobs that need information analysis skills is five million within the U.S.A. alone. You've got an opportunity to grab these opportunities. You simply would like the proper skills. square measure you fluent in activity information analysis, exploitation spreadsheets, programming, decoding statistics, management, big data, machine learning, and prophetical analytics?

Corporations rate their hour groups low on analytical skills. There merely are not enough folks that possess these skills to require on data-driven jobs. A study shows that solely eighteen of hour professionals presently have these skills. it is also projected that the talent gap can continue to grow.

The University of California estimates that the world demand for information scientists has already exceeded the provision by over five hundredths. It's no secret that information, digitization, and analytics have become crucial. it's vital to understand-How digital hour capabilities amendment individuals management? according to the 2016 survey, it discovered that about to 1/2 enterprises studied forty seventh still suppose paper-based methods for compensation activities forty second still use paper for international grading and job leveling and twenty eighth still suppose paper for a few performance management tasks suggests that that way too several hour departments square measure stuck managing manual methods that embrace paper forms and manual approvals hour work is troublesome enough to make sure the correct talent is known and also the best individuals square measure within the proper positions the power to fast move throughout the continued process of recruiting hiring on boarding advantages and even off-boarding needs economical handling of knowledge of info and quick deciding digital hour facilitates to alleviate frustration once individuals processes and aims square measure reaching a world pool of talent to urge the most effective indicative however will digital hour help beloved it pushes corporations to be a lot of data-driven foundational advanced and transactional analytics supply the power to act on data-driven information higher target worker wants and perceive this hands in real time variety 2 it streamlines the choice and hiring process thinning out the time needed to urge approvals for indicative means longer spent distinguishing new talent and coaching current talent variety 3 it improves the standard of labor life when hiring is complete hour can specialize in making certain active engagement and participation in an exceedingly culture that's free from negativity with digital hour processes hour managers can specialize in integration interaction association and analytical thinking to make sure the most effective individuals get the foremost work done effectively to seek out the advantages of human capital management and digital hour processes. One recently announced that working from home is there to stay even post-COVID. Microsoft has also unveiled plans to adopt a hybrid workplace, which offers employees greater flexibility once the pandemic subsides- Rethinking HR.

A logical consequence of the increase in at-home workers apart from a spike in office furniture sales and Zoom accounts is the push for HR to rethink many of its practices. Activities like recruiting, onboarding, performance management, and even firing decisions have relied on in-person conversations. HR needs to reinvent current practices to effectively deal with these situations in a digital world. More fundamentally, the way we have designed and structured our organization will have to change.

Many companies have already made use of online tools to foster a culture of togetherness, despite the physical distance. Virtual happy hours have started to replace after-work socializing. Regular departmental check-ins have become increasingly important. In the coming year, we may see companies beginning to test additional virtual structured experiences to simulate the camaraderie and exploration that was once only possible organically. -

Reinventing the employee experience. The differences between joining an organization pre-COVID and during COVID are huge. From a people perspective, the company focuses on learning, listening, and empathy building, and they actively work to create a service mindset for their team members. Other interventions include value-based recruitment. Organizations that do this assess to what degree the values of a candidate align with their organizational values. HR professionals play an important role in integrating these practices and then continuously reinforcing them and show the potential of Digital Transformation in the Human Resources Domain.

CHAPTER TEN

Supply Chain

Supply chain management: is an integral part of all the industries around the Globe major transformations have been going on in various industries but this has caused a growing concern for the environment this has led to the adoption of green supply chain management in various industries and has grown in popularity over the last few years the practice is used in many business sectors government education service and manufacturing many companies have increased their consciousness of the world's environmental problems that exist such as using toxic substances increasing global warming and decreasing the earth's resources the government on many occasions has promoted the awareness of these problems organizations on the other hand have applied green principles to their company and his processes things such as using environmentally friendly materials recycling products reducing or deleting the usage of certain chemicals and using alternative environmentally safe products the green practices expanded the departments within the organization including the supply chain both internally and externally one definition of green supply chain management is the alignment of sourcing manufacturing distribution transportation and remanufacturing / recycling processes with the goal of reducing a company's carbon footprint. Green supply chain management integrates environmental thinking into the supply chain including material sourcing design manufacturing logistics and even end-of-life management after the product has become obsolete there are many benefits of using GCM concepts within an organization. The two most common are reducing the consumption of toxic chemicals in less waste other benefits include sustainability of Natural Resources lowering costs increased efficiency product differentiation brand reputation reducing risk employee morale and the ethical imperative of conserving the environment the implementation of Green and sustainable supply chain starts at the daily operation level of the organization simple tasks like recycling can we implement in every department within the organization when thinking of the supply chain. It starts with the designing of the product when designing a product engineering has to change the raw material specifications and also focus on less toxic substances used during the manufacturing stage of the process in manufacturing the company can focus on reducing energy and resource consumption along with implementing reuse and recycle processes purchasing can go green by focusing on environmental initiatives and encouraging suppliers to do the same some of the initiatives can include renewable energy usage reduction of waste and use of more environmentally friendly products. Therefore, it is important to stress the benefits of having the practices in place the popularity of implementing "G SCM" (Green and Sustainable Supply Chain) which is growing with the awareness of preserving the environmental cost and time to implement a green supply chain.

Every action in this world has two sides: But is that true for green supply chain management too? While green supply chain management indeed has a positive impact on the environment, companies use this concept to kill two birds with one stone because a green supply chain can not only help reduce production costs and pollution it can also spur economic growth provide better opportunities to sell products or services in a pro-environment atmosphere and provide a competitive advantage with regards to a positive image increased reputation and greater customer satisfaction it gives a win-win situation for both the companies implementing it and the environment the significant positive impacts of embracing a green supply chain management are as follows minimize pollution obviously adopting green supply chain practices helps companies minimize the detrimental impact their supply chain has on the environment this can be achieved by designing products in such a way that it minimizes pollution and energy minimizing pollution is also achieved by the adoption of lean policies which leads to the elimination of costly losses that affect the financial health of the company and also maximize profits. This green supply chain practices inadvertently end up reducing the cost of operations and thus improve the financial health of the company. Measures have been taken by different businesses and companies who are looking for ways to reduce their impact on the environment and approaches that will only continue to grow as it becomes more cost-effective. Green supply chain management provides the use of alternative fuels and the establishment of local relationships with suppliers to implement this strategy some companies will need to downsize and purchase items from a few sources they should consider how they can tailor their products and packaging to accommodate new suppliers improvising transportation arrangements can create many difficulties most modern transportation methods release emissions to some extent and green alternatives aren't always widespread or accessible green materials sustainable materials that reduce resource depletion lower acquisition costs and reduce carbon emissions examples of construction in textile industries include bamboo tencel linen and cork each material is renewable or requires little energy to harvest and build the energy associated with an asset is directly related to how much is needed to make it from purchase to refinement green manufacturing reduces the combined energy thereby reducing the environmental impact detoxification is part of the "G SCM" that reduces the presence of toxic substances reverse logistics it addresses how companies handle products once they have achieved their goal grain supply chain management promotes reuse and recycling although products may be subjected to other disposal measures if they are not reused companies refer to this strategy as a closed-loop system that incorporates materials that go out and return for repurposing customers return detective or recycle products to their manufacturer which becomes either waste products or new products by adopting these six ways firms improve their performance by improving product quality and improving service delivery it has made many corporate active contributors to ecological preservation and conservation such as reducing carbon emissions and eliminating waste from the supply chain they have increased their bottom lines by dialing back on wasteful practices and investing those costs in high quality product management.

Conclusion: Therefore, Sustainability is becoming less of a good to have and more of a must to have for businesses in their supply chains there are ways to reduce your carbon footprint in the supply chain that has a positive impact on the environment as well because the current practices are not sufficient enough to meet both ends of the business world that is the environmental sustainability and business profitability in future due to further advancement in technology the green supply chain management practices might be capable of achieving this balance.

Impact of Industry 4.0 on Supply Chains

The supply chain is the processes from the initial raw material to the ultimate consumption of the finished product linking across the supplier using company or is the function within and outside company that enabled a value chain to make product and provide service to the customer. Supply chain management performance has a direct on the organization's overall performance from the cost control perspective is estimated the companies with an extended global supply chain have between 80 and 90 percent of their cost tie-up. The complexity of the modern supply chain caused by the global omnichannel distribution and widespread market means supply chain management is an essential customer has become more demanding to have a stop of what they went or we move on costing lost. E.g. if customers order items online, they expect on-time delivery and is rewritten process for unwanted purchases many manufacturers are dependent on just in time when statistically delivery of components not only on time but also not before time and in exactly the required quantity of mentioned retailers have to figure out the best way to combine the sometimes conflicting demand of being a motive store and online retail businesses meet flexible and adaptable supply chains they can respond quickly to capitalize on opportunities offered by rapidly changing customer practice this is the basic supply chain management.

The supply chain management in industry 4.0 is a means for the current trend of automation and data exchange in manufacturing technology it includes cyber-physical system Internet of Things cloud computing and 3d printing in the steel revolution 4.0 fist what has been called Smart Factory so this is industrial 4.0. It is imperative to understand each component of the supply chain management process.

For the **first component** planning and execution phase in supply chain management focused on end to end process and maintaining a balance between supply and demand position and are more data-driven and the integration of Ultimi end-to-end data aggression solution will be a game-changer in saying the more practical approach the integration and digitization of operation eliminate sizes in enterprise allowing decision-makers across function to respond to the disruption in real-time weather is a shortage of raw materials the thing to change in market dynamic or customer preference identify the root cause of inefficiency in the day-to-day operation or gathering much intelligence to plan for the future.

The **second component** procurement and manufacturing as the monomer manufacturing holding capacity and the current supply landscape this are some of the factors that affect procurement and this operation over here the integration of life demand data from current performance and inventory data from manufacturing and holding facilities as well as up-to-date information on the in-transit raw material of entry from suppliers can help streamline procurement and manufacturing operations to be the point where buffer or safety stock is no longer necessary industry 4.0 is all about digitization and the integration of monetary drinking and analytics technologies to enable seamless supply chain management and input operational efficiency both now and in the future for the existing processor.

For the **third component** logistic and transportation management by far has the most to gain from supply chain digitization industry 4.0 the ultimate real-time management of lack of shipments and infill effects like shipping containers is going to be improving productivity real-time shipment tracking solution will allow supply chain managers to optimize routes and fill asset utilization in real-time with the added advantage of automation to reduce the need for human intervention automate logistic management system improve responsiveness to change the effect throughout and ancestry overhead like real cost and the ability to hit narrowing windows of delivery. For the last component, the housing industry 4.0 warehouse will function as an autonomous entity with automation handling the majority of tasks like space management inventory tracking and ordering, simplifying or reducing labor-intensive tests can move efficiency and reduce operational overhead when coupled with end-to-end supply chain visibility solution for inbound or outbound logistics my warehouse can anticipate the inflow of goods and space requirements the question except like personal openness and update Enterprise electric holding and throughput level in real-time warehouse event retracting and management systems coupled with other emerging technologies like augmented reality could also be an option to increase process efficiency.

In the conclusion, industry 4.0 on the digital supply chain is not limited to efficiency, but the supply chain digitization solutions will give customer's an edge over competitors improve the ability to service customers and build better business collaboration and generate more avenues for revenue early text monster and implement by the project to completely transform digital supply network to manage the cost of time.

CHAPTER ELEVEN

Shaping the Future of Work

The world is undergoing fundamental and disruptive changes like technological, organizational, climatic which are presenting new challenges to the future of work. These global megatrends have a profound impact on skills. Many of the skills of today will not match the jobs of tomorrow and the skills learned today can quickly become obsolete. The concept of lifelong learning has been around for decades, and the ILO has adopted numerous normative instruments and policies related to lifelong learning. But the unprecedented transformation that is taking place is redefining its terms and giving it new importance. International agencies like the United Nations Agenda for Sustainable Development and the Global Commission on the Future of Work have called for formal recognition of entitlement to lifelong learning. Ultimately, lifelong learning remains the key for people to be able to benefit from modern ways of working. And it will light the path on our journey to a more promising future of work because this world of work is changing radically.

If we talk about the other aspect of the prospect, the transition in technology can be more successful for women for which they need more and different skills. In mature economies like Canada, the United Kingdom, and the United States, the only net job growth may be in jobs requiring a college or advanced degree. In emerging economies like India, many women working in subsistence agriculture with little education and low skills may find it hard to find work in other sectors that require both. In terms of equality women in many regions of the world especially in emerging economies, lag behind men in educational attainment. Women tend to be less mobile than men. Therefore, it is the technology that will give women the flexibility and new ways to make a living. Through which they can be successful in the automation era, but they will need concerted help and creative new solutions to help them thrive in the work of the future. In terms of technology, the emerging allocation technologies and machine tools will improve our productivity because the skill sets of the future being things like creative problem solving and working with people, and very important emotional intelligence and self-efficacy. These skill sets that we are looking for are ones essentially that the robots can't do. Bring creativity and humanness into the workforce. What comes through in the evidence is the next generation of skills needed for future jobs. Those skills are often about synthesis and judgment. They are about creativity and problem solving and are often about interacting with others and collaborating with others to solve problems, and they are fundamentally human skills, so they are the very characteristics that won't be replaced by machines. There is no doubt that people will be adapting and needing new skills, the rate of change, rather than being in a steady-state, is now exponential. Resilience and adaptability are just critical. The underpinning of excellence in everything is an explorer. Be a teacher, be a university professor, a politician, they're charting new frontiers, pushing the boundary of knowledge, setting new standards and best practices, and that's what an explorer is. The science and the curiosity of asking these questions is a fundamental aspect of human biology in nature. The amount of new information and techniques and research questions that we can ask now is at a scale that we'd never seen before in human history. People should not consider artificial intelligence is not a threat because there is a rare case where people need to be proactive in regulation instead of reactive. At present humans have machine learning algorithms that can solve an incredibly complex problem beyond any human intelligence as they are mere machines that can be given enormous data set and they come up with brilliant correlations and insights but they're not going threaten the human population anytime soon because fish intelligent isn't terrible but a human being a smart enough to learn that skills at least to have a complete toolbox to be prepared volatility of the future adaptability. Thus, the first phase of the internet remains a nervous system, where humans could sense what was going on in other nodes - the people connected. In the second phase, we discover we can perform functions in the real world by cooperating as biological multicellular organisms once discovered. The difference between a superorganism and a real organism is we keep our individuality; there is no principal unit taking decisions on behalf of all of us, we are all free. However, the Covid-19 has reshaped the world in ways that will endure long after the pandemic ends and has affected future job opportunities. Remote work is here to stay. E-commerce is soaring. Automation is accelerating. Our research indicates the mix of available jobs will change as a result, creating more urgency for instructing workers for the changes ahead. More than 100 million workers in our focus countries or one in 16 may need to switch occupations by 2030. Job growth will be more heavily concentrated in high skill jobs, while middle and low skill jobs decline. The explosion in e-commerce set off a scramble for unlikely warehouse workers to stop. Investment in the green economy will increase the need for wind turbine technicians. The demand for photographers could increase to meet our increasingly visual means of communication. Aging populations in many advanced economies will increase the demand for nurses, home health aides, and hearing aid technicians. Teachers and training instructors will also continue finding work over the coming decade.

But the forces unleashed by COVID-19 have put other jobs at risk. Business travel is unlikely to recover quickly. And that affects flight attendants, airline mechanics, and baggage handlers. The use of self-checkout stands accelerated during the pandemic, displacing some grocery store clerks. Companies have deployed robotics to process routine paperwork, replacing office workers. We are entering an era of occupational transitions, an era that demands answers to questions about the alternative approaches to training that can support the millions of people making these transitions. To protect the social fabric and benefits, like sick leave and unemployment insurance, are needed for all workers, including gig workers? Can business and government leaders come together to generate solutions, not only for navigating the pandemic but for navigating the post-pandemic world of work, because, for the millions of workers already in vulnerable situations, the COVID-19 crisis has had devastating consequences. It has led to increases in forced labor, child labor, and discrimination, and the denial of freedom of association and collective bargaining in many workplaces. Preserving and strengthening these fundamental rights at work is critical to protecting the most vulnerable and building more resilient, equitable, and productive societies after the pandemic. Extending income support for workers helps reduce the risk of forced labor. Safeguarding children's education prevents the most vulnerable from falling into child labor. Ensuring inclusiveness in the crisis response can help mitigate discrimination in employment. Giving workers a voice through freedom of association and collective bargaining leads to better, negotiated policy solutions to the crisis. "Leaving no one behind" means putting the most vulnerable at the center of the COVID-19 response and protecting fundamental principles and rights at work.

Therefore, the future of work is in the hands of the humans and not on the technology or the pandemic, we are the ones who need to cooperate and make sure that we work in peace and harmony because "Work is worship" will be a false statement. And it is not the robots who will impact our jobs" but the humans will.

Workplace Wellness: Performance with a Purpose

When we talk about, workplace health, from the perspective of employers. Workplace health includes, providing the conditions, for personal development, and allowing individuals, to become the best they can be, thanks to the opportunities available to them, in the workplace. When the employer says that - "If we give you everything you need, to do your job, properly or if we keep your working environment safe, we are ensuring, workplace health. When we talk about, workplace health, from the perspective of the employees. We are talking about, a function of emotional health well-being and happiness, and in the workplace. So, when employees say that, we can take care of our physical health, it is much more, a function of psychological and emotional health, and social health, than it is of physical health because good emotional health comes from, working in a respectful place. When we talk about, good emotional health from a perspective of an employee is about a place where we are essentially talking about, feeling respected, feeling valued, feeling emotionally comfortable, in the workplace, etc.

At the same time, it is imperative to understand the factors or elements, that affect workplace health. The first one is organizational culture. Organizational culture refers to, the social setup, within an organization.

Interpersonal relationships within an organization. The way of working, in an organization. The stories, that propagate, the way of working, the hours. All of that constitutes the organizational culture of the systems, everything. What kind of system of rewards, do you have in your organization? The other is the promotion. Health promotion programs, that are conducted by the organization, for its employees. And physical amenities. What you have. What you deal with. You know, your employee lounge, your gym, your places for a walk, etc. Then the flexibility of the workplace is another factor, The amount of control, you have over your job. If you are a very rule-driven, instruction-driven, person, then flexibility could confuse you. But, if you are an independent thinker. If you are, and you know, both have merits. We need very instruction-driven people, for very high-risk jobs. Because, unless things are done, with an enormous amount of precision, you just cannot do, which you are required to do. The option is to be flexible with the workplace, either in terms of resources or time or contribution. But, over and above that, if there is some flexibility, that always helps is Communication. The Perceived ease of communication with superiors and subordinates. However, the most important factor is the management support which depends upon how much does the organization support you, in your attempts to grow, in your attempts to do, what you are required to perform. How much, do they trust your integrity, is what, management support means. How much, do they support you, in terms of, training needs, or the personal goals, with the organizational goals, etc.

According to **research**, 28 percent of adults are not thriving in any element while just 19 are thriving in four or five elements employees with low well-being are the source of immense health care costs and lost productivity for organizations there are a few ways that organizations can invest in their employee's well-being and encourage participation in well-being programs first communicate clarify that well-being is an important organizational value second individualize let employees choose well-being activities that are best suited to their individual wellness goals and interests and third recognize understand that recognition reinforces your well-being efforts successful wellness programs focus on providing the tools resources and opportunities to develop and strengthen each of the five areas of total employee well-being understand that every person is different so your program needs to be tailored to meet employees needs interests and goals. In recent times, with the coming up of Covid-19, the world is learning new ways to live life and build community and work, which can increase feelings of frustration, anxiety and stress.Organizations need to lead thinking about mental health by creating a supportive space for teams.Before Covid, nearly 60% of employees didn't tell anyone at work about their mental health.Many do not know what resources are available or are afraid to use them.

To **conclude**, organizations need to ensure their employees understand the mental health benefits and resources available. Be specific: phone numbers and websites. Reiterate organizational support. And lead by

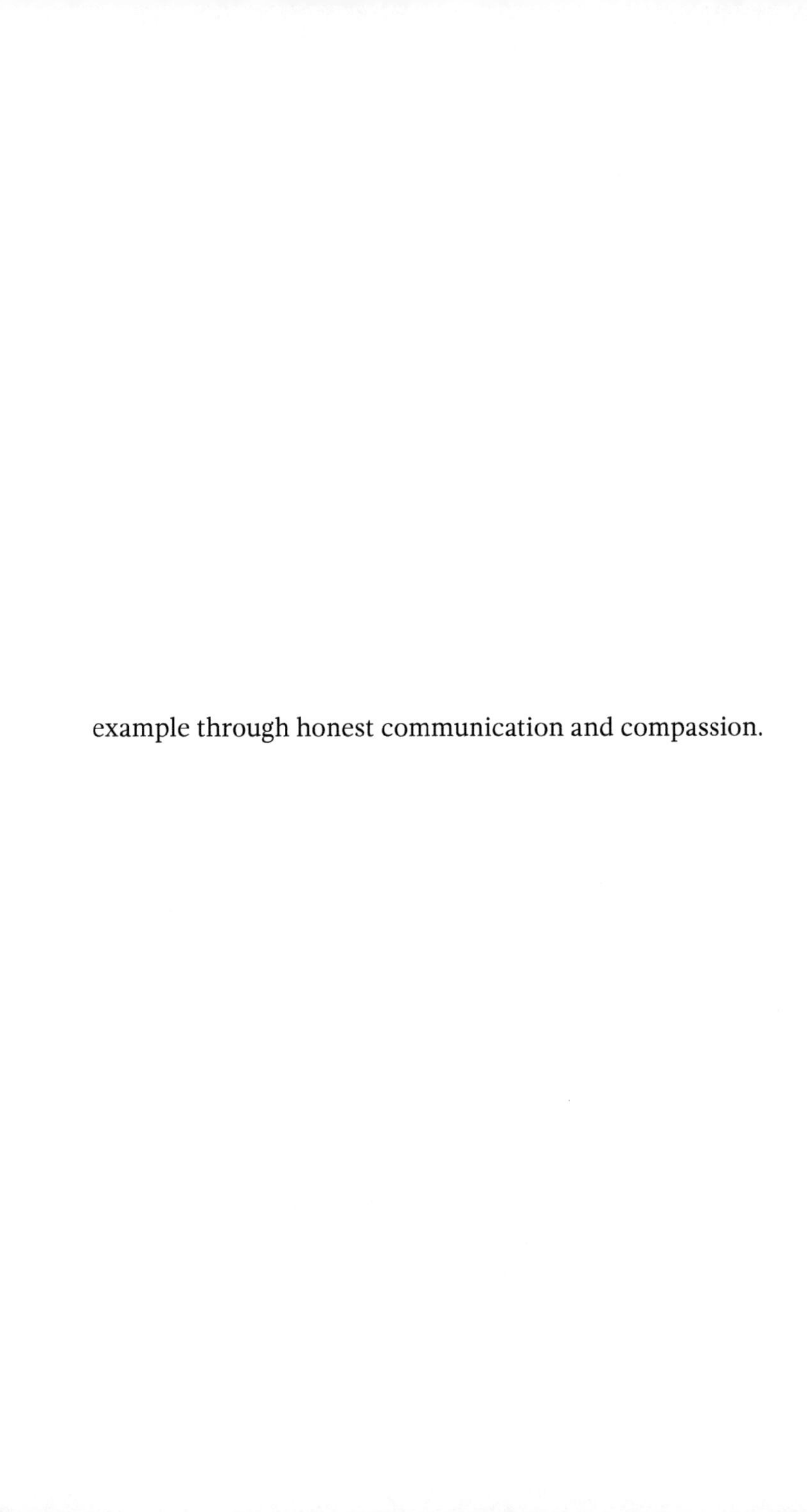

example through honest communication and compassion.

21st century is in the hands of Hard workers or Smart workers

Work is important to succeed as it is a stepping stone to the next level of success the most relevant question is about the kind of work that will take one to that level is it hard work or is it smart work. A hard worker is a person who worked towards what he observes to be worth striving for regardless of how compelling the situation might be a success for hard work doesn't occur overnight but only after embedding in long hours at work and depriving oneself of the pleasures of life it's not working a smart a worker is a person who works towards what he sees to be worth striving for and utilizes his brain and efforts in the most effective manner with the help of integration of both it ensures prosperous results with least human energy wasted. As Lots of people work hard but only if you become successful and this is where smart work appears in and to start tugging in as a smart worker there is an essential rule you need to keep in mind the value of what you create isn't about how much work went into it it's estimated by how useful it is to oneself so if you can get the same result and generate something of value by putting in less effort and time then that's the path one should be taking and shouldn't feel embarrassed about doing less work to get there it'll mean the time effort and other resources one saved can all be put to far better use on the face of it seems obvious but it's something a lot of people could be doing better.

How to define hard work, when we have to handle several tasks, mostly in our adept fields we have to work hard as well as smart, and anything created on the establishment of hard work is long-lasting and reliable but at times it may become monotonous and wearisome as hard work doesn't allow you to fully use your brain and it pushes you for more substantial work if we fail after doing so much hard work it becomes difficult to cope, while Smart work helps you to find the source of the problem and helps to cut its time management skills as it is it's just about mere efficiency, The most prominent life management skill is time management that smart workers are very well aware that time is the most valuable resource they have they value their time the most in their lives the smart workers learn to maintain their time wisely value investing and can sink in opportunities, for example, to push a dice if you only had a sphere you'd make things move 20 times faster a lot of people spend ages trying to figure out how to turn the dice into a ball but the smart way isn't to try doing this because either it's improbable or it will take a huge amount of work the smart way is to try and carry the dice yet a lot of people don't figure this out and spend way too long trying to turn the dice into a sphere instead of searching for sphere just outsource a carriage even if it comes at a price you'll still be able to carry more cubes pay for the cart and still make a profit, thus, smart workers are very careful to select the possibilities they engage with they have no difficulty in saying no they are steady and wait for the one right thing with a massive potential return this is called value spending and your time is the most expensive resource that you can invest your potential and resources.

There is a quote implying that "**hard work is the key to success**"- that is quite true, but not entirely true in the era of smart phones and gadgets. Everyone needs an easy way to perform their work, merely few people look for an effective way. Working smart is required, whereas it would be half-done if you don't work hard. And one of, the best ways to complete a task is to use knowledge, your intelligence. Smart work is more prolific. first of all, smart work does not mean you do not work hard, it means before you start to do one thing, you should think sensibly about what is the best way to accomplish this goal, what is the most efficient way to be more lucrative on short time related to the people who work a long time but less productive., secondly, smart work builds people who can be more innovative. the digital era evolves so fast there was a time when some people always want to improve the traditional old working way to find a faster, more effective, and more innovative way to work. so it can be concluded that smart work is the outcome of people's intellect. Only you put the smart work first, then the hard work can be significant. This is the basic difference between smart work and hard work. Smart work means using your efforts to their maximum benefit. It doesn't mean simply distancing yourself from hard work but executing the right choices. It means holding your head with you. See to be successful; one had to give some points to prove. But the difference lies in where. Smart worker plans and puts in efforts to fields that will generate good and a hard worker well simply work hard which means that you put long hours into work while working smart means to truly maximize your effort being the most effective you can be despite the number of ampere-hours you work per day. Reaching the top of your field demands working hard.

However, you also need to be resilient and flexible to the benefits of the technology. That's what working 'smart' basically means these days. one needs to be accomplished, and performance comes with sources. Which, today, the tech industry has full custody of. "Many people work hard but only a few become prosperous." That's right. It's just because working hard is not always sufficient. So, what's their secret? There are, in fact, components of smart work you can perform the 'working hard' approach and style to develop. The more components you insert, the more intelligent you will begin to achieve. Some of the major components of the 'smart' work are: Appropriate timing, Having authority over things, Know the system you are in, that's why it becomes imperative to always look on the golden side as the Bottom line is, nowadays problems that arise with this dichotomy are that we all too frequently frame this as a choice where one should only choose one or another. It is either 'hard' or 'smart'. The truth is that Work Smart, not hard" is one of those self-help truisms that is hard to deny because like most self-help truisms it says nothing provocative and nothing beyond plain-vanilla common sense. Of course, it is better to work smart.

Why in the wide world would one want to work simply hard, when working smartly is a possible option?

The main problem is that most self-help analogy is fact that it has unintended consequences. This work-smart mania has two primary fall-outs; it has generated a huge audicence for people who plan work schedules, planning frameworks, and the like for others. These people will then take up a lot of other people's time; time which if used usefully otherwise might have been way more useful than anything else. A large number of people spend more and more time waiting for inspiration and to arrive at the best way of doing things. Instead of just doing the required thing. The conclusion fruits of toil smart work are the fruit of hard work and to understand the traits of smart work one needs to work hard in the beginning planning.

The planning is the biggest difference but in hard work and smart work without proper strategy or planning whatever you do the probabilities of success will always below the planning be based upon the reality and on the ground level of the situation based upon the situation, one needs to find out the easiest way out of a demanding problem. As hard work never bothers about that but smart work can make a way to handle a complicated problem in an easier way determining to work smart a simple way to turn hard work into smart work is by knowing the aftermath of the process if one keeps on working without reliable results then they should try working smartly rather than concentrating all the attention on the work think about all the alternatives that could be undertaken to do the equal amount of work in less time thus if one can merge working hard and smart together, will achieve great heights and eat yourself to a better future.

Therefore, one who works hard and smart will in due course of time to get all the benefits and will lead to the path of true success.

CHAPTER TWELVE

Globalization and Business

Going beyond the basic definition of globalization, it can be understand with the case study of China. As the one belt one road is an ambitious project initiated by the Chinese president.

The two main objectives are the :-

a) Silk Road economic belt and

b) the maritime silver which consists implementation of railways ports roads

Along with other infrastructure projects the enlarged cooperation and connectivity with Eurasia. The subject matter of connectivity is the stimulate trade and exports with China's neighbors increase the popularity of their currency or maybe and increase export demand for Chinese capacities as high emphasis on Eurasia and a Southeast Asia for various reasons such as Eurasia's proximity to western china accessing the enriched natural resources and most importantly to make up region stability similarly Southeast Asia is prioritized because of the strategic location for trade opportunities the maritime route is expected to be developed later since China faces obstacles in establishing sea routes and opposition's from many countries because of China's policy towards the South China Sea China's GDP per capita is largely lowered compared to its GDP per capita is largely lower compared to its potential partners due to the international challenges such as the regional development gap between disparate locations within the country people living below the poverty line continues migration from the countryside to the major cities the vital industry over capacity and the difficulty in employment that young graduates face.

The increases in infrastructure is the main part of one build one Road and the main purpose is to increase the tip trade flows along the Silk Route both and in order to do this there's a five trillion US dollar investment needed. Furthermore at a schedule that the project is going to finish in a 2049

The five main areas of infrastructure that will be improved is roads telecommunication electricity gas and oil and Maritime

Manufacturing will increase the export demand for construction it will increase export demand for engineering and even though it's the export demand which might sound a bit fun it's actually China that is going to supply most of the label that is going to be used for the projects also those projects not going to be built within China furthermore this is going to reduce the Chinese oil capacity which has been a huge problem during the recent years so a wall it's going to highly positively affect the Chinese business environment and especially manufacturing if we then look on the African business environment that the story is not entirely the same because China's largest funder of infrastructure in Africa and China is also the main builder of infrastructure in Africa this means that even though the projects are going to be built in Africa it's actually Chinese workers who are building it so it's a negative effect for Africa but once again it's very positive for China furthermore there's been a lot of public-private partnerships between Chinese companies and the African government and not all of these has been entirely after the book because there's been a lot of concern because many of these does not have open and public tender rings and this is again hurting the African business environment next if we look at transport and logistics there will be a huge demand for transportation and logistics which will increase this is of course very positive then there's going to be a lot of raw materials needed in order to build infrastructure so again the transportation of these the demand will also increase and then there will also be a increased distribution centers in the Asian region because you need to be able to quicker get out to the desired markets for the more freedoms look at China then there's going to be a lot of logistics ups for example Hong Kong can really utilize the logistics experience and become one of the main suppliers of knowledge about logistics within one belt one Road China has invested heavily in making Shang Shu a global logistics hub and have now open trade routes from there to Germany and many other places furthermore China beliefs and expects that at least for in Chinese cities will become huge statistics

The Problem Ahead For China:

China's largest banks are raising billions of dollars from on and offshore investors finally these large-scale infrastructures require costly investments high standards of management and long operating cycles all of which translate in a great uncertainty in the project's profitability my legal and regulatory risk point of view unfairness and corruptions are two major risk the project concurs in some countries this has been proven by unfair rulings in the local courts and contract negotiations can also be linked to the projects at risk local stability is also a risk as many countries in which opera projects are implemented are subject to political instability and protests in some countries could impact the government's attitude towards foreign investments as they may choose to adopt a more nationalist approach to the flag popular anger before making investment decisions political in stable countries Chinese enterprises must also consider whether there will be significant changes in ruling governments as they may potentially lead to huge losses terrorism is also a major risk. The durability of infrastructure risk is due to most investments being made in emerging economies with ethnic tension and territorial claims this makes the building of infrastructure of honored blown and stable own has sometimes resulted in costly failures and non profitable projects in the long run because of the size and extent of the project there is also a strong social risk as the project will result in the removal and marginalization of local communities and ethnicities the supposedly important economic benefits brought on by these projects are also unclear to whether the gains will be inclusive from an environmental point of view this project causes destruction of wildlife and protected areas and creates a lot of pollution many countries also means different regulations regarding environmental issues and investors should pay sufficient attention to these regulations as environmental protection issues could trigger crisis and even lead to investment failures finally the labor market risk is linked to the poor working condition for their migrants and construction workers and some countries also face a shortage of skilled labour for the project and to compensate they will need to import skilled specialists however it is consequently rises the cost of production.

There are four important outputs to the future that will be affecting the global markets firstly the middle-income being our countries are expected to see growth in power rail and healthcare the power consumption is trailing the GDP per capita and a substantial increase in power projects are expected because the government's aspired to close the supply gap furthermore beyond our countries lagging behind the railway network have the motives to integrate their large territories with the rail route also countries with fast-growing populations are not in step with the hospital capacity additions so high investments are expected in these RMB countries secondly the transfer Asian rail network will enable the fight time to significantly decrease and create economic integration between the world's most populated regions thirdly due to the population growth and urbanization that will be high demand for capacity transportation infrastructure last the over will most likely give rise to the popularity of rain moving geopolitics creates major obstacles for over since Eurasia is currently in a state of crisis and Central Asia is one of the world's most politically unstable locations so these factors causes disagreements between China and BNR countries which don't add up to a promising market for Chinese goods for this reason China's intentions of finishing over with success is not guaranteed and is still debatable process this is humor speaking robot will bring a lot of positive effects for the business environment in many different sectors especially in China is going to increase demand and many different sectors however there's also a lot of risk combined with Uber and there is a huge need for transparency in the communication if it is to succeed if it is to succeed there will be a lot of increased trade along the route which will benefit most of the countries involved.

CHAPTER THIRTEEN

The Present Covid Scenario

Resilience is defined as the process of adapting excellently in the face of adversity. Trauma, tragedy threats are significant sources of stress. Developing an increased capacity to identify other sources of stress promotes resilience. For people, resilience means you rebound rather than falling apart. After a crisis like work conflicts or financial setbacks, resilience won't eliminate risk or rectify your problems instead provides an opportunity and clarity to see past them while better managing your stress levels. However, terms of business resilience refer to "the ability to recover from or adjust easily to misfortune or change". Business resilience is the ability an organization has to quickly adapt to disruptions while maintaining continuous business operations and safeguarding people, assets, and overall brand equity. Business resilience planning is also frequently referred to as business continuity planning and is an assessment of the sustainability of a given organization. Even before COVID-19, many businesses were struggling to plan for, respond to, resume speed, and keep pace with technological change, but with the advent of covid 19, this pandemic has changed consumer behavior.

Because of this pandemic, most of the nations worldwide have opted for a nationwide lockdown. Businesses are put up in shatters, which affected economies in many countries. Nearly all types of businesses have been negatively impacted by this outbreak and continue to do so as workforces dwindle because of high infection rates. The hardest-hit large and medium scale business was logistics. With nearly 75% of companies witnessing or forecasting a disruption in their supply chain, lead times have doubled, and limited freight options by any route have made things worse.

The need for resilience can be comprehended from a survey conducted in 2020 which indicated that around 800 employees from public, private and nonprofit firms about what was happening in their lives that required resilience. What did they determine? They didn't point to tragedies or the economy. They pointed to corporate culture and their coworkers. Understanding that in times like these, the key to moving forward is thinking positively albeit difficult, and becoming resilient. An important element of business resilience is how sustainable companies would weather a storm, how they prepared for them, how they acted during tougher phases, and how they came out of them. Most of these organizations relying absolutely on data analytics and automation. It became comprehensible that digital technologies will prove to remain an increasingly critical element of business resilience which ensures business: One: exist in a growing market, two: focus on recurring revenues, three: don't rely on loopholes, four: automate numerous human activities, five: focuses on high ticket sales, and six: deliver results fast. Whether or not, resilience represents the key to longevity, scalability, and ultimately the success of your business.

Business resilience focuses on implementing digital systems and processes to ensure business continuity, while offering products or services that remain, or will become, desirable in the face of global events, financial instability, or threats to a business's core operations. The Resilient people possess three characteristics, the staunch acceptance of reality, a deep belief often buttressed by strongly held values, that life is meaningful and an uncanny ability to improvise. Resilient people and companies face reality with staunchness, make meaning of hardship instead of crying out in despair, and improvise solutions from thin air "So as sure as the sun will shine, I'm going to obtain my share now of what's mine. And then the harder they come, the harder they'll fall, one and all. The final strategy and the one that increases the effectiveness of both of the prior strategies is client acquisition automation. In general, there are three distinct stages of client acquisition, each of which can substantially improve with automation y creating a safety buffer by cleaning up their balance sheets before the dip. Two, most companies cut costs ahead of the curve. And three, they focused on growth, even if it meant incurring costs.

Thus, business resilience is based upon 3c's method that includes the community where one has to look out for not just yourself your company your organization but the community as well in the messaging that you're sending especially during a covid crisis.

Second, The confidence you have to be calm but not Stillwater calm. One has to project confidence that they are going to be able to see this through successfully with the minimum amount of hurt to the company but also to all of the stakeholders who are relying on the leadership to get them through the difficult days and months ahead number and third, the collaboration. You are not going to know all the answers no one expects you to this is a time for you to call on the resources the capabilities of all of your employees all of your team members and bring them together in task force's sub-task forces have everyone potentially given a role in which they feel they can be contributing to overcoming the uncertainty overcoming the crisis engaging a lot of your employees in this way will also reduce the rumor mill give confidence to them that they will then project and turn to the people who are relying on them as their managers for direction so collaboration teamwork delving into your organization.

Therefore, a life crisis is inevitable and the exclusive way to implement these strategies and to overcome the crisis is through resilience. Thus, Resilience is that ineffable quality that allows some people to be knocked down by life and come back stronger than ever. Rather than allowing failure to overcome them and drain their resolve, they find a way to rise from the ashes.

CHAPTER FOURTEEN

The Roadmap

Roadmap are important because the margin of error for most startups is small founders use our roadmap to help form and shape plans for their startup the info graphic is built upon a framework which is a business planning process that stands for vision strategy execution and metrics is often used by experienced executives to figure out where they need to go and to develop strategies execution tasks and metrics that take them there this info graphic focuses on the vision and high level concepts most founders should start by understanding the business journey for their startup which begins with the parallel tasks of forming your startup and validating your idea.

The second phase is validating your model the key task of this phase is achieving product market fit many entrepreneurs tend to conclude that they've reached product market fit before they actually have the third phase is to establish traction it's important to have a strong metrics infrastructure to show and prove your traction which will help convince investors employees and partners that your startup has momentum the fourth phase is to build out your infrastructure which is all about building the foundation needed to effectively scale the company in phase.

The companies that have successfully built scale are prime candidates for a nice exit when you look at the critical success factors for a startup it's important to start with validation because seventy percent of all startups fail due to premature scaling that means companies built too much of their product or spent too much on marketing or ramped up their staffing too quickly before they validated their business model in phase two having this roadmap will help you to execute well which is an important part of building a fundable startup.

In order to build a fundable startup before you try to raise funds on your funding journey each round of fundraising should be synchronized with your company's inflection points as that anchors your funding strategy which is how you maximize your startup payout .This roadmap is to illustrate the key phases of a startup's development so founders can assemble the right team to execute the right tasks at the right time .Therefore, this team should deploy solid methodical and defensible plans to build and grow a healthy startup.

Impact of Budget 2022 on Diffrent startups

The 1st big development was hinted at by the finance minister in her Budget speech which involve the PM GatiShakti program. It is expected to help develop the national infrastructure for the next 25 years andpave the way for a multimodal transport network across India.

The Gatishakti plan will be animated by 7 engines that are:Routes, railways, airports, ports, mass transportation, navigation and logistics infrastructure.The plan aims to advance economic transformation through seamless multimodal connectivity and logistics efficiency.

Under this plan, a master plan for Expressways will be made in 2022-23. And the National Highways network will be expanded by 25,000 km with funds of Rs 20,000 Cr being set aside for these plans.Contracts will also be allocated to the implementation of multimodal logistical parks in four positions via PPP mode during the year. Around 400 Vande Bharat trains will be developed and built over the next 3 years. The Gatishakti freight terminals for multimodal logistical services have been developed for being developed three years. Financing and faster implementation of Metro systems will also be implemented according to the plan. These initiatives have added to the other CAPEX announcements. They have resulted in a sharp rise of over 35% in the Capex outlay for FY23 which has risen to Rs 7.5 Lac Cr vs Rs 5.54 Lac Cr last year. The continued announcement of these massive infrastructure plans has seen infrastructure stocks like- L&T & IRB Infra ending the day at above 3% gain. Cement makers like Shree Cement & Dalmia Bharat have seen a 5%+ gain today. Ultratech, India Cements, Ramco, and JK Lakshmi have all seen gains of above 3%. Even metal stocks like Tata Steel, Jindal Steel, and Vedanta have rallied 5-7.5% today highlighting the positive impact of these announcements on the sector

The 2nd big development was the announcement of the Central Bank Digital Currency of Digital Rupee. This is expected to provide a big boost to the digital economy. Highlight the stance of the authorities in exploring blockchain technologies and practically implementing them in the country. Digital rupee should be released during the year of the RBI. Regarding digital assets, the FM has also announced a brand-new taxation scheme for virtual digital assets. It is proposed that any income from the transfer of any virtual digital activity is taxed at a fixed rate of 30%.

Further details regarding this new tax regime are:

Losses from this asset class will not be used to offset profits from other asset classes. TDS of 1% will be deducted at the time of the transaction. Gifting of these assets will also be taxed at the same 30%, This development may be a downer for virtual digital investors in the short term. But it highlights the increasing acceptance of virtual assets like cryptocurrencies and NFTs in India.

The 3rd big development was regarding clean energy and electric vehicles space. The FM has proposed the creation of special mobility zones in urban areas under development. These zones shall be used exclusively for public transport using clean energy and electric vehicles. FM stated that given the constraint of space in urban areas for setting up charging stations at scale, the goverment will be bringing in a battery swapping policy officially and will formulate interoperability standards to support this movement.

It is also expected to encourage the development of battery or energy as a service model for the private sector. Battery Swapping is a mechanism in which instead of using a fixed immovable battery structure that can only be charged at a charging point, consumers can use portable batteries where low-charge batteries can be exchanged with fully charged batteries for a fee. In the clean energy space, the FM has proposed the target of making 280 GW of installed solar capacity by 2030 aided by an additional allocation of Rs 19,500 crore for the Solar Cell PLI scheme. These announcements resulted in minor rises in the prices of battery makers like Exide, Amara Raja, And stocks associated with solar energy like Adani Green Energy and Borosil Renewables.

The 4th big announcement was regarding the housing sector in India.FM announced that +80 Lac houses will be completed for identified eligible beneficiaries of PM Awas Yojana in rural and urban areas. Around Rs. 48,000 Cr will be allocated for this program this year. Furthermore, an allocation of Rs 60,000 Cr has also been made to provide access to tap water to 3.8 Cr households under the Har Ghar, Nal Se Jal program which is also expected to benefit the affordable housing sector immensely. This announcement saw Affordable Housing players rise with AAVAS Financiers shooting up almost 10% HDFC Ltd and Canfin Homes have both seen gains of over 1.9% today. These announcements were also partly responsible for the gains seen in the cement and steel sectors which were the biggest gainers in the market today.

The 5th big announcement was the extension of additional credit to the MSME sector under the Emergency Credit Line Guarantee Scheme The government has extended ECLGS to March 2023. The guaranteed cover has expanded by Rs 50,000 Cr to a total of Rs 5 Lac Cr. But it is a big relief for the MSME sector, it is expected to lead to higher NPAs in public sector banks in the future when the program winds up. This expectation saw a big divergence emerge in the banking sector stocks with private banks rising while public sector banks have fallen. It resulted in the Nifty Private Bank index rising 1.93%, Nifty PSU Bank index had fallen 0.58% by the end of the day. The 6th and last big development of the day was the absence of any changes to the income tax regime. The only major development regarding income tax was that taxpayers can now file an Updated Return on payment of additional tax.This updated return may be filed within two years from the end of the corresponding evaluation year.

Another development of note here was that the surcharge on Long Term Capital Gains on the sale of unlisted assets was capped at 15% from the previous 37% at its peak. This surcharge is an additional charge levied above the LTCG on the sale of any long-term asset of big transaction size. The surcharge followed a slab structure where the % charged increased with transaction size. The highest slab for listed assets like equity and fixed income is already fixed at 15%. For unlisted assets like property, it was as high as 37% for gains above Rs five Cr. This is the figure which has been reduced by the government to only 15% bringing the LTCG treatment for both listed and unlisted assets at par and incentivizing the long-term holding of assets. Although this is of little consequence for everyday investors, we thought to clarify this point completely so that there isn't any misconception that the actual LTCG has increased to 15% from the actual 10%.

Therefore, Budget 2022 has not delivered on the expectation of income tax relief, there have also been no negative developments regarding taxation and in most of the important points, the status quo has been maintained.

The End....

This book provides an overview of business and finance as it relates to sustainablity,development and other important areas of growth. It also provides a roadmap to recent trends in the field of finance and accounts. It also talks about the importance of workplace wellness and Supply chain management performance which has a direct on the organization's overall performance from the cost control perspective is estimated the companies with an extended global supply chain along with the role of women in the field of business and trading. India has traditionally been a patriarchal society with low participation of women in the economy. But the fact remains that women represent nearly 50 percent of the total population, and it is crucial to encourage women's role in the economy at every level. The entrepreneurial role is limited to large-scale industries and technology-based businesses. The book also provides strategic resilience during the Pandemic whcich is dynamic and Flexible planning for business improvements. The business quadrant shows the different methods by which income is generated. Various income generation methods require unique or particular technical skills, training courses and different types of people. And it's a useful tool that led entrepreneurial paths of ambitious people in the search for financial freedom. Thus, the book is a cluster of diffrent articles which aims to provide a deep understanding on the very nature of business and its impact on the society.

www.ingramcontent.com/pod-product-compliance
Ingram Content Group UK Ltd.
Pitfield, Milton Keynes, MK11 3LW, UK
UKHW021936190726
13853UKWH00004B/1485